cooking
curries

cooking
curries

MURDOCH BOOKS

contents

a world of flavour

For such a humble sounding word, 'curry' refers to some of the world's most delicious and popular dishes. The word itself was first coined by the British in India, possibly deriving from the Tamil word *kari*, meaning 'spiced sauce'. Today the term covers dishes that range from simple to sophisticated, complex to singularly bold, those that can be made in minutes or left for hours over a bed of coals, and includes the everyday food of peasants to the once-exclusive creations of the rich and royal.

Use of the word has expanded to include the curries of Southeast Asia alongside those of India, and this book features dishes from cuisines as varied as those of Kashmir, Goa, Bangladesh, Thailand, Malaysia, Sri Lanka, Laos and Vietnam. Despite this diversity, all curries share a few essential elements: a curry paste, seasonings — which can vary from fresh herbs to pungent shrimp paste — and the 'main' ingredient, such as meat, fish, pulses or vegetables. From there, curries can go in many directions. They may be dry, oily, wet, thick or thin. The cooking can involve frying, boiling, steaming or slow, gentle braising. Adjectives such as sour, salty, hot, sweet, creamy, pungent and fragrant may all be applied to a finished dish, more often than not in combination. In fact, if anything unites curries, it is their skill in blending various tastes, textures and aromas to create superb dishes of great depth and balance.

The essential starting place is the curry paste. The paste will infuse the other ingredients with its flavour and fragrance, and its creation is a real part of the pleasure of making a curry. Traditionally, curry pastes are made by hand, the ingredients added one-by-one to a mortar for grinding or to the frying pan for roasting, with the cook observing, smelling and adjusting as necessary. Buying prepared spice mixtures is convenient, but to experience the real thing, have a go at preparing one from scratch.

Of course, the other thing that unites curries is rice. This staple of life is central to the cuisines of India and Southeast Asia, and curries are there to support the rice — not the other way round. Once again, the trick is to seek balance, combining delicately perfumed rice with vegetable dishes, side dishes and curries to match. This book contains some classic raitas, pickles and breads to experiment with and many more wonderful curries that amply demonstrate the delight to be found in this age-old dish.

rich

Creamy, smooth curries are often the best place to start if new to curries. In fact, many of the world's favourite curries belong to this type — the most common examples include butter chicken, Thai musaman beef curry, Indian lamb kormas and the many kofta, or meatball, recipes that are served resting on a bed of rich, creamy sauce. These curries have coconut milk, ground nuts, yoghurt or cream as their base, sometimes singly but often in combination.

Coconut is perhaps the most versatile of these products. It harmonizes flavours, subdues the potency of fiery chillies and balances sour ingredients such as Thai apple eggplants (aubergines), tart lime juice and salty shrimp paste. The taste of the coconut itself is also important. Fresh coconut cream, in particular, enriches the curry with its own depth of flavour, so that dishes are complex and sumptuous — not merely creamy.

Tinned coconut cream does not have the same qualities as fresh coconut but is much easier to obtain, so the recipes in this chapter presume the tinned variety will be used. Many of the recipes ask that you do not shake the tin, as the thick cream on the top can be used to fry the paste, with just a little oil added. The coconut cream may also need to be simmered before adding the curry paste. This is done so that most of the water evaporates and the cream becomes quite oily, ensuring that the curry paste is fried, not boiled.

Many of the dishes in this chapter come from tropical areas of India and Thailand, where coconut trees flourish. Every part of the tree is used, from thatching for houses to making lotions for the skin and hair from the oil. In India, coconut forms the basis of golden, thick korma-style curries, perfected by the Moguls in the seventeenth century, as well as the yoghurt-based dumpling dishes of Gujarat and the spicy seafood curries of coastal Goa. Thai uses of coconut are just as varied and delicious. Their spicy red curries, the sharp green curries and the panaeng and musaman curries of the south all have coconut as their starting point.

In contrast to coconut, yoghurt is more often used as a thickener and tenderizer of meat than as a flavouring, producing wonderfully tender, slow-cooked curries of lamb and beef. It is also the key ingredient in soothing Indian raitas, for which many of us have been thankful.

thai beef and peanut curry .... serves 4–6

LIKE ALL THAI CURRIES, THE KEY TO THIS DISH IS BALANCE: IT HAS A SWEET, SPICY AND SALTY PASTE COMBINED WITH THE RICH SMOOTHNESS OF PEANUTS AND COCONUT. CHOOSE A BEEF CUT THAT WILL BENEFIT FROM SLOW COOKING. TO ROAST THE PEANUTS YOURSELF, COOK AT 180°C (350°F/GAS 4) FOR 8–10 MINUTES, OR UNTIL GOLDEN.

curry paste

dried long red chillies	8–10
red Asian shallots	6, chopped
garlic	6 cloves
ground coriander	1 teaspoon
ground cumin	1 tablespoon
ground white pepper	1 teaspoon
lemon grass	2 stems, white part only, sliced
galangal	1 tablespoon chopped
coriander (cilantro)	6 roots
shrimp paste	2 teaspoons
roasted peanuts	2 tablespoons
peanut oil	if needed
coconut cream	400 ml (14 fl oz)
	(do not shake the tin)
round or blade steak	1 kg (2 lb 4 oz), thinly sliced
coconut milk	400 ml (14 fl oz)
makrut (kaffir lime) leaves	4
crunchy peanut butter	90 g (3¼ oz/⅓ cup)
lime juice	3 tablespoons
fish sauce	2½ tablespoons
palm sugar (jaggery)	2½ tablespoons shaved
Thai basil	optional, to serve
roasted peanuts	1 tablespoon chopped, optional, to serve

Soak the chillies in boiling water for 5 minutes, or until soft. Remove the stem and seeds, then chop. Put the chillies and the remaining curry paste ingredients in a food processor, or in a mortar with a pestle, and process or pound to a smooth paste. Add a little peanut oil if it is too thick.

Put the thick coconut cream from the top of the tin in a saucepan, bring to a rapid simmer over medium heat, stirring occasionally, and cook for 5–10 minutes, or until the mixture 'splits' (the oil starts to separate). Add 6–8 tablespoons of the curry paste and cook, stirring, for a further 5–10 minutes, or until fragrant.

Add the beef, the remaining coconut cream, coconut milk, makrut leaves and peanut butter, and cook for 8 minutes, or until the beef just starts to change colour. Reduce the heat and simmer for 1 hour, or until the beef is tender.

Stir in the lime juice, fish sauce and palm sugar, and transfer to a serving dish. Garnish with the basil leaves, and extra peanuts, if desired.

Remove the stem and seeds and chop the softened chillies.

Use a food processor to process the paste ingredients quickly.

pork curry with eggplant ....serves 4

PORK IS A FAVOURITE MEAT ACROSS MUCH OF INDIA AND SOUTHEAST ASIA, BUT IS USED IN RELATIVELY FEW CURRIES. WHEN IT IS USED, IT IS OFTEN TEAMED WITH OTHER RICH FLAVOURS, SUCH AS COCONUT. DON'T RUSH THIS DISH, AS THE SLOW, GENTLE COOKING ENSURES THE MEAT IS VERY TENDER.

curry paste

long red chillies	4, split lengthways, seeded
galangal	1 thick slice, chopped
spring onion (scallion)	1, chopped
garlic	2 cloves, chopped
coriander (cilantro)	2 roots, chopped
lemon grass	1 stem, white part only, thinly sliced
ground white pepper	1 teaspoon
shrimp paste	1/2 teaspoon
fish sauce	1 teaspoon
crunchy peanut butter	2 tablespoons
pork shoulder	600 g (1 lb 5 oz)
ginger	1 thick slice
palm sugar (jaggery)	2 tablespoons shaved
fish sauce	80 ml (2 1/2 fl oz/1/3 cup)
coconut cream	400 ml (14 fl oz) (do not shake the tin)
eggplant (aubergine)	250 g (9 oz), cut into 2 cm (3/4 in) cubes
bamboo shoots	225 g (8 oz) tinned, drained, sliced, or 140 g (5 oz) drained
Thai basil	1 large handful, chopped

Put the split chillies in a shallow bowl and pour over enough hot water to just cover and rest for 15 minutes, or until softened. Drain, reserving 1 tablespoon of the soaking liquid.

Put the chillies and reserved soaking liquid with the remaining curry paste ingredients, except the peanut butter, in a food processor, or in a mortar with a pestle, and process or pound to a smooth paste. Stir in the peanut butter.

Cut the pork into 1 cm (1/2 in) thick slices. Put in a saucepan and cover with water. Add the ginger slice, 1 tablespoon of the palm sugar and 1 tablespoon of the fish sauce. Bring to the boil over high heat then reduce to a simmer and cook for 20–25 minutes, or until the meat is tender. Remove from the heat and allow the meat to cool in the liquid stock. Then strain, reserving 250 ml (9 fl oz/1 cup) of the cooking liquid.

Put the thick coconut cream from the top of the tin in a saucepan, bring to a rapid simmer over medium heat, stirring occasionally, and cook for 5–10 minutes, or until the mixture 'splits' (the oil starts to separate). Add the curry paste and remaining palm sugar and fish sauce, and bring to the boil. Reduce to a simmer and cook for about 3 minutes, or until fragrant. Add the pork, eggplant, sliced bamboo, the reserved pork cooking liquid and the remaining coconut cream. Increase heat and bring to the boil again before reducing to a simmer and cooking for a further 20–25 minutes, or until the eggplant is tender and sauce has thickened slightly. Top with the basil leaves.

Split the chillies then scrape away the seeds with a knife.

Stir the peanut butter into the paste, mixing until smooth.

musaman vegetable curry . . . . serves 4–6

THIS CURRY IS A GOOD ONE TO TRY IF YOU ARE NEW TO CURRIES. IT IS SUMPTUOUSLY SPICED AND SEASONED WITHOUT BEING FIERY OR OVERLY RICH, AND HAS A LIGHTNESS OF FLAVOUR NOT SEEN IN MANY MEAT CURRIES. SIMILARLY, THE SAUCE IS THICK, NEITHER TOO WET NOR DRY, AND PERFECT FOR SCOOPING UP WITH RICE OR BREAD.

musaman curry paste

oil	1 tablespoon
coriander seeds	1 teaspoon
cumin seeds	1 teaspoon
cloves	8
fennel seeds	1/2 teaspoon
cardamom seeds	4
red Asian shallots	6, chopped
garlic	3 cloves, chopped
lemon grass	1 teaspoon finely chopped, white part only
galangal	1 teaspoon finely chopped
dried long red chillies	4
ground nutmeg	1 teaspoon
ground white pepper	1 teaspoon
oil	1 tablespoon
baby onions	250 g (9 oz)
baby new potatoes	500 g (1 lb 2 oz)
carrots	300 g (10 1/2 oz), cut into 3 cm (1 1/4 in) pieces
baby button mushrooms (champignons)	225 g (8 oz) tinned, whole, drained
cinnamon stick	1
makrut (kaffir lime) leaf	1
bay leaf	1
coconut cream	250 ml (9 fl oz/1 cup)
lime juice	1 tablespoon
palm sugar (jaggery)	3 teaspoons shaved
Thai basil	1 tablespoon finely chopped, plus extra to serve
roasted peanuts	1 tablespoon crushed

Heat the oil in a frying pan over low heat, add the coriander seeds, cumin seeds, cloves, fennel seeds and cardamom seeds, and cook for 1–2 minutes, or until fragrant.

Put the spices with the remaining curry paste ingredients in a food processor, or in a mortar with a pestle, and process or pound to a smooth paste. Add a little water if it is too thick.

Heat the oil in a large saucepan, add the curry paste and cook, stirring, over medium heat for 2 minutes, or until fragrant. Add the vegetables, cinnamon stick, makrut leaf, bay leaf and enough water to cover (about 500 ml/17 fl oz/2 cups), and bring to the boil. Reduce the heat and simmer, covered, stirring frequently, for 30–35 minutes, or until the vegetables are cooked.

Stir in the coconut cream and cook, uncovered, for 4 minutes, stirring frequently, until thickened slightly. Stir in the lime juice, palm sugar and chopped basil. Add a little water if the sauce is too dry. Top with the peanuts and basil leaves.

thai red duck curry with pineapple . . . . serves 4–6

THE ART OF THAI CURRIES — AND THE REASON WHY WE KEEP COMING BACK TO THEM — IS THE WAY THEY COMBINE DIFFERENT FLAVOURS AND TEXTURES IN THE ONE DISH TO CREATE A HARMONIOUS WHOLE. THIS DISH IS A PERFECT EXAMPLE OF THAT SKILL; BLENDING SWEET, SAVOURY AND SPICY INGREDIENTS WITH RICH COCONUT MILK.

red curry paste

dried long red chillies	15
white peppercorns	1 tablespoon
coriander seeds	2 teaspoons
cumin seeds	1 teaspoon
shrimp paste	2 teaspoons
red Asian shallots	5, chopped
garlic	10 cloves, chopped
lemon grass	2 stems, white part only, finely sliced
galangal	1 tablespoon chopped
coriander (cilantro)	2 tablespoons chopped root
makrut (kaffir lime) zest	1 teaspoon finely grated
peanut oil	1 tablespoon
spring onions (scallions)	8, sliced on the diagonal into 3 cm (1 1/4 in) lengths
garlic	2 cloves, crushed
Chinese roast duck	1, chopped into large pieces
coconut milk	400 ml (14 fl oz)
pineapple pieces in syrup	450 g (1 lb), tinned, drained
makrut (kaffir lime) leaves	3
coriander (cilantro)	3 tablespoons chopped leaves
mint	2 tablespoons chopped

Soak the chillies in boiling water for 5 minutes, or until soft. Remove the stem and seeds, then chop. Dry-fry the peppercorns, coriander seeds, cumin seeds, and shrimp paste wrapped in foil in a frying pan over medium–high heat for 2–3 minutes, or until fragrant. Allow to cool. Using a mortar with a pestle, or a spice grinder, crush or grind the peppercorns, coriander and cumin to a powder.

Put the chopped chillies, shrimp paste and ground spices with the remaining curry paste ingredients in a food processor, or in a mortar with a pestle, and process or pound to a smooth paste.

Heat a wok until very hot, add the oil and swirl to coat the side. Add the onion, garlic and 2–4 tablespoons made red curry paste, and stir-fry for 1 minute, or until fragrant.

Add the roast duck pieces, coconut milk, drained pineapple pieces, makrut leaves, and half the coriander and mint. Bring to the boil, then reduce the heat and simmer for 10 minutes, or until the duck is heated through and the sauce has thickened slightly. Stir in the remaining coriander and mint, and serve.

fish and peanut curry . . . . serves 6

ONE OF THE STAR INGREDIENTS IN THIS DISH IS CRISP FRIED ONION, WHICH CAN BE BOUGHT FROM ASIAN FOOD STORES, OR EASILY PREPARED AT HOME (SEE NOTE BELOW). AS WELL, DRIED SPICES AND SOUR TAMARIND ARE USED TO NICELY BALANCE THE CREAMY, NUTTY FLAVOURS OF THIS DISH.

sesame seeds	50 g (1³/4 oz/¹/3 cup)
cayenne pepper	¹/2 teaspoon
ground turmeric	¹/4 teaspoon
desiccated coconut	1 tablespoon
ground coriander	2 teaspoons
ground cumin	¹/2 teaspoon
crisp fried onion	40 g (1¹/2 oz/¹/2 cup)
ginger	5 cm (2 in) piece, chopped
garlic	2 cloves, chopped
tamarind purée	3 tablespoons
crunchy peanut butter	1 tablespoon
roasted peanuts	1 tablespoon
curry leaves	8, plus extra, to serve
skinless, firm white fish fillets	1 kg (2 lb 4 oz), cut into 2 cm (³/4 in) cubes
lemon juice	1 tablespoon

Put the sesame seeds in a heavy-based frying pan, over medium heat, and stir until golden. Add the cayenne pepper, turmeric, coconut, ground coriander and ground cumin and stir for a further minute, or until aromatic. Set aside to cool.

Put the fried onions, ginger, garlic, tamarind, 1 teaspoon salt, peanut butter, roasted peanuts, sesame spice mix and 500 ml (17 fl oz/2 cups) hot water in a food processor and process until mixture reaches a smooth, thick consistency.

Put the sauce and curry leaves into a heavy-based frying pan over medium heat and bring to a simmer. Cover and simmer over low heat for 15 minutes, then add the fish in a single layer. Simmer, covered, for a further 5 minutes, or until the fish is just cooked through. Gently stir through the lemon juice, and season well to taste. Garnish with curry leaves and serve.

Note: To make crisp fried onion at home, very thinly slice 1 onion, then dry on paper towel for 10 minutes. Fill a deep, heavy-based saucepan one-third full of oil and heat to 160°C (315°F), or until a cube of bread dropped into the oil browns in 30 seconds. Fry the onions for up to 1 minute, or until crisp and golden. Drain well, cool and store in an airtight container for up to 2 weeks. Use as a garnish and flavour enhancer for curries, rice and noodle dishes.

Stir the sesame seeds over medium heat until lightly golden.

Add the spices to the frying pan and stir until aromatic.

Add the fish in a single layer to the simmering sauce.

three ways with rice

IT IS IMPOSSIBLE TO OVERESTIMATE THE IMPORTANCE OF RICE FOR THE PEOPLES OF SOUTHEAST ASIA AND INDIA. INDEED, CURRIES ARE THERE TO SUPPORT THE RICE, NOT THE OTHER WAY AROUND. RICE IS COMBINED WITH INGREDIENTS RANGING FROM THE MOST HUMBLE TO THE MOST LUXURIOUS. SAFFRON, THE WORLD'S MOST EXPENSIVE SPICE, IS USED TO FLAVOUR INDIAN AND PERSIAN RICE DISHES, SUCH AS PILAFF AND BIRYANI, WHILE OTHER STAPLES SUCH AS LENTILS AND COCONUT ARE ALSO COMMON, AND DELICIOUS, ADDITIONS TO RICE.

saffron rice

Wash 400 g (14 oz/2 cups) basmati rice, cover with cold water and soak for 30 minutes, then drain. Melt 25 g (1 oz) butter in a frying pan over medium heat then add 3 bay leaves and the drained rice. Cook, stirring, for 6 minutes, or until all the moisture has evaporated. Meanwhile, soak $1/4$ teaspoon saffron threads in 2 tablespoons hot water for a few minutes then add to the rice with 500 ml (17 fl oz/2 cups) boiling vegetable stock, 375 ml (13 fl oz/1$1/2$ cups) boiling water and salt to taste. Bring to the boil, then reduce the heat and cook, covered, for 12–15 minutes, or until all the water is absorbed and the rice is cooked. Serves 6.

seasoned rice and lentils

Wash 300 g (10$1/2$ oz/1$1/2$ cups) basmati rice and 300 g (10$1/2$ oz/1$2/3$ cups) split mung beans (mung lentils) then drain and set aside. Heat 2 tablespoons oil in a frying pan, add 1 sliced onion, 3 bay leaves, 1 teaspoon cumin seeds, 2 pieces cassia bark, 1 tablespoon cardamom seeds, 6 cloves and $1/4$ teaspoon black peppercorns and cook over low heat for 5 minutes, or until the onion is softened and the spices are fragrant. Add the rice and lentils, and cook, stirring, for 2 minutes. Pour in 1.25 litres (44 fl oz/5 cups) water and salt to taste. Bring to the boil, then reduce the heat and cook, covered, over low heat for 15 minutes. Stir gently to avoid breaking the grains and cook, uncovered, over low heat for 3 minutes, or until all the moisture has evaporated. Discard the whole spices when the dish is cooked. Serves 6.

coconut rice

Rinse 400 g (14 oz/2 cups) long-grain rice and cover with 1 litre (35 fl oz/4 cups) water. Set aside for 30 minutes then drain. Bring 750 ml (26 fl oz/3 cups) water to the boil. Add the rice, 1 pandanus leaf tied in a knot and salt to taste. Reduce the heat and cook, covered, for 12 minutes, or until the rice is just cooked. Remove from heat and add 185 ml (6 fl oz/$3/4$ cup) coconut cream. Stir gently to avoid breaking the grains. Cover and set aside for 10 minutes, or until the rice absorbs the coconut cream in the residual heat. Discard the pandanus leaf before serving. Serves 6.

saffron rice

lamb shank and yoghurt curry . . . . serves 6

THIS IS NOT A CURRY TO MAKE AT THE LAST MINUTE, BUT THE SLOW COOKING PRODUCES WONDERFULLY TENDER MEAT, WHILE ALSO ALLOWING FOR THE SUBTLE AROMAS AND FLAVOURS OF THE SPICES TO EMERGE AND BLEND. LAMB SHANK IS IDEAL FOR THIS AND THE USE OF YOGHURT THICKENS THE SAUCE AND ROUNDS OFF THE DISH.

coriander seeds	3 tablespoons
cumin seeds	2 teaspoons
cloves	1 teaspoon
black peppercorns	1 teaspoon
cayenne pepper	1/2 teaspoon
ground turmeric	1 teaspoon
ginger	2 tablespoons chopped
garlic	6 cloves, chopped
onion	1 small, chopped
ghee or oil	2 tablespoons
lamb shanks	6
cinnamon sticks	3
bay leaves	2
plain yoghurt	375 g (13 oz/1 1/2 cups)
chicken stock	625 ml (21 1/2 fl oz/2 1/2 cups)

Preheat the oven to 160°C (315°F/Gas 2–3).

Dry-fry the coriander seeds, cumin seeds, cloves, peppercorns, cayenne pepper and ground turmeric in a frying pan over medium–high heat for 2–3 minutes, or until fragrant. Allow to cool. Using a mortar with a pestle, or a spice grinder, crush or grind to a powder.

Put the ground spices with the ginger, garlic, onion and 3 tablespoons water in a food processor, or in a mortar with a pestle, and process or pound to a smooth paste.

In a large heavy-based frying pan, heat the ghee or oil over medium–high heat and brown the shanks in batches and set aside. Reduce the heat to low. Add the ginger spice paste to the frying pan, and cook for 5–8 minutes. Add the cinnamon, bay leaves and yoghurt to the pan, a spoonful at a time, stirring well so it incorporates smoothly. Add the chicken stock and stir well to combine.

Put the shanks into a large heavy-based ovenproof dish that will fit them in a single layer, then pour the yoghurt sauce over the top of the shanks. Turn the shanks so they are coated with the sauce, and cover with a lid, or foil. Bake in the oven for about 3 hours, or until the lamb is falling from the bone, turning the shanks halfway through cooking. When you remove from the oven, skim any oil that comes to the surface and discard.

Remove the shanks from the sauce onto a serving platter. Season the sauce well to taste, stirring to mix before spooning over the shanks.

thai red beef curry
with thai eggplants .... serves 4

THERE ARE MANY VARIATIONS ON THE BASIC RED CURRY, BUT ALL ARE DISTINGUISHED BY THE DARK SHADE OF
THE SAUCE. THE COLOUR, OF COURSE, COMES FROM A GOOD DOSE OF DRIED LONG RED CHILLIES IN THE PASTE.
MOST RED CURRIES ARE WET (NOT DRY), AND FRAGRANT WITH FRESH MAKRUT (KAFFIR LIME) AND THAI BASIL.

round or topside steak	500 g (1 lb 2 oz)
coconut cream	250 ml (9 fl oz/1 cup)
	(do not shake the tin)
red curry paste	2 tablespoons, ready-made or
	see recipe on page 18
fish sauce	2 tablespoons
palm sugar (jaggery)	1 tablespoon shaved
makrut (kaffir lime) leaves	5, halved
coconut milk	500 ml (17 fl oz/2 cups)
Thai apple eggplants	
(aubergines)	8, halved
Thai basil	1 small handful, finely shredded

Cut the meat into 5 cm (2 in) pieces, then cut across the grain at a 45° angle into 5 mm (¼ in) thick slices.

Put the thick coconut cream from the top of the tin in a saucepan, bring to a rapid simmer over medium heat, stirring occasionally, and cook for 5–10 minutes, or until the mixture 'splits' (the oil starts to separate). Add the curry paste and simmer, stirring to prevent it sticking to the bottom, for 5 minutes, or until fragrant.

Add the meat and cook, stirring, for 3–5 minutes, or until it changes colour. Add the fish sauce, palm sugar, makrut leaves, coconut milk and remaining coconut cream, and simmer for 1 hour, or until the meat is tender and the sauce slightly thickened.

Add the eggplant and cook for 10 minutes, or until tender. If the sauce is too thick, add a little water. Stir in the basil leaves and serve.

This tropical Asian fruit comes in an array of shapes, sizes and colours that would surprise most people. In Thailand alone, popular eggplant (aubergine) varieties include long, skinny, pale green ones — similar to purple Japanese baby eggplants, but milder — as well as Thai apple eggplants (confusingly, the size of golf balls), which are full of seeds and can be quite bitter. Both have specific uses in Thai cooking: the former in green curries and grills, and the latter in salads, curries and relishes. Other varieties are the sour-tasting fuzzy eggplants and pea eggplants. This last type grows in clusters and is bitter-tasting, but is valued precisely for that quality. They are sometimes available pickled in jars.

rich chicken koftas . . . . serves 4

KOFTA MIGHT CONTAIN MEAT, FISH OR VEGETABLES BUT ALL ARE WELL-COMBINED MIXTURES, WITH ADDED HERBS AND
SPICES. ACCOMPANYING SAUCES ARE EQUALLY APPEALING —— IN THIS DISH, THE SAUCE IS RICH WITH COCONUT,
YOGHURT, CREAM AND ALMONDS, BALANCED BY THE SPICY, PEPPERY NOTES OF GARAM MASALA AND TURMERIC.

koftas

oil	2 tablespoons
onion	1, finely chopped
garlic	1 clove, crushed
ginger	1 teaspoon finely chopped
ground cumin	1 teaspoon
garam masala	1 teaspoon
ground turmeric	1/2 teaspoon
chicken thigh fillets	650 g (1 lb 7 oz), trimmed
coriander (cilantro)	2 tablespoons chopped leaves
onion	1, roughly chopped
ghee or oil	1 tablespoon
garlic	2 cloves, crushed
garam masala	2 teaspoons
ground turmeric	1/2 teaspoon
coconut milk	170 ml (5 1/2 fl oz/2/3 cup)
plain yoghurt	90 g (3 1/4 oz/1/3 cup)
cream (whipping)	125 ml (4 fl oz/1/2 cup)
ground almonds	35 g (1 1/4 oz/1/3 cup)
coriander (cilantro)	2 tablespoons chopped leaves

To make the koftas, heat half the oil in a frying pan. Add the onion, garlic, ginger, ground cumin, garam masala and ground turmeric, and cook, stirring, for 4–6 minutes, or until the onion is tender and spices are fragrant. Allow to cool.

Put the chicken fillets in batches in a food processor and process until just chopped. Do not over-process the mixture.

Put the chicken, onion mixture, coriander and 1/2 teaspoon salt in a bowl, and mix together well. Using wetted hands, measure 1 tablespoon of mixture and shape into a ball. Repeat with the remaining mixture. Heat the remaining oil in a heavy-based frying pan, add the koftas in batches and cook for 4–5 minutes, or until well browned all over. Remove from the pan and cover. Put the onion in a food processor and process until smooth.

Heat the ghee or oil in a frying pan. Add the onion and garlic, and cook, stirring, for 5 minutes, or until the onion juices evaporate and the mixture starts to thicken. Add the garam masala and turmeric, and cook for a further 2 minutes. Add the coconut milk, yoghurt, cream and ground almonds. Gently bring almost to the boil, then reduce the heat to medium and add the koftas. Cook, stirring occasionally, for 15 minutes, or until the koftas are cooked through. Stir in the coriander and serve.

Mix the chicken, onion mixture, coriander and salt together.

Use wetted hands to shape the chicken mixture into balls.

Fry the chicken koftas in batches and remove from the pan.

lamb korma..serves 4

A FAMILIAR STAPLE OF INDIAN RESTAURANTS AROUND THE WORLD, KORMA IS MORE THAN A DISH — IT IS A COOKING STYLE. PUT SIMPLY, IT CONSISTS OF MARINATED MEAT OR VEGETABLES THAT ARE COOKED WITH GHEE OR OIL, THEN BRAISED WITH WATER OR STOCK, YOGHURT OR CREAM (OR SOMETIMES ALL OF THESE).

lamb leg meat	1 kg (2 lb 4 oz)
onion	1, chopped, plus 1 sliced
ginger	2 teaspoons grated
garlic	4 cloves
ground coriander	2 teaspoons
ground cumin	2 teaspoons
cardamom seeds	1 teaspoon
cloves	1/4 teaspoon
ground cinnamon	1/4 teaspoon
long green chillies	3, seeded, chopped
ghee or oil	2 tablespoons
tomato paste (concentrated purée)	2 1/2 tablespoons
plain yoghurt	125 g (4 1/2 oz/1/2 cup)
coconut cream	125 ml (4 fl oz/1/2 cup)
ground almonds	50 g (1 3/4 oz/1/2 cup)
toasted slivered almonds	to serve

Trim any excess fat or sinew from the lamb, cut into 3 cm (1 1/4 in) cubes and put in a large bowl.

Put the chopped onion, ginger, garlic, coriander, cumin, cardamom seeds, cloves, cinnamon, chilli and 1/2 teaspoon salt in a food processor, or in a mortar with a pestle, and process or pound to a smooth paste. Add the spice paste to the lamb and mix well to coat. Leave to marinate for 1 hour.

Heat the ghee or oil in a large saucepan, add the sliced onion and cook, stirring, over low heat for 7 minutes, or until the onion is soft. Increase the heat to medium–high and add the lamb mixture and cook, stirring constantly, for 8–10 minutes, or until the lamb changes colour.

Stir in the tomato paste, yoghurt, coconut cream and ground almonds. Reduce the heat and simmer, covered, stirring occasionally, for about 1 hour, or until the meat is very tender. Add a little water if the mixture becomes too dry. Season well with salt and pepper, and serve garnished with the slivered almonds.

Add the spice paste to the lamb and leave to marinate.

Add the lamb mixture to the pan and cook until it changes colour.

scallops and prawns chu chee .... serves 4

CHU CHEE CURRY PASTE IS THE TRADITIONAL THAI FLAVOUR BASE FOR SEAFOOD. IT IS SIMILAR TO A RED CURRY PASTE, IN THAT DRIED RED CHILLIES DOMINATE, BUT THE PROPORTION OF AROMATICS SUCH AS GALANGAL, LEMON GRASS, MAKRUT (KAFFIR LIME) LEAVES AND CORIANDER (CILANTRO) ARE GREATER.

chu chee curry paste

dried long red chillies	10
coriander seeds	1 teaspoon
shrimp paste	1 tablespoon
white peppercorns	1 tablespoon
makrut (kaffir lime) leaves	10, finely shredded
red Asian shallots	10, chopped
makrut (kaffir lime) zest	2 teaspoons finely grated
coriander (cilantro)	1 tablespoon chopped stem and root
lemon grass	1 stem, white part only, finely chopped
galangal	3 tablespoons chopped
krachai	1 tablespoon chopped, optional (see note)
garlic	6 cloves, crushed
coconut cream	540 ml (18½ fl oz) (do not shake the tins)
scallops	500 g (1 lb 2 oz), with roe removed
raw king prawns (shrimp)	500 g (1 lb 2 oz), peeled, deveined, tails intact
fish sauce	2–3 tablespoons
palm sugar (jaggery)	2–3 tablespoons
makrut (kaffir lime) leaves	8, finely shredded
red chillies	2, thinly sliced
Thai basil	1 large handful

Soak the chillies in boiling water for 5 minutes, or until soft. Remove the stem and seeds, then chop. Dry-fry the coriander seeds, shrimp paste wrapped in foil, and peppercorns in a frying pan over medium–high heat for 2–3 minutes, or until fragrant. Allow to cool. Using a mortar with a pestle, or a spice grinder, crush or grind the coriander and peppercorns to a powder.

Put the chopped chillies, shrimp paste and ground coriander and peppercorns with the remaining curry paste ingredients in a food processor, or in a mortar with a pestle, and process or pound to a smooth paste.

Put the thick coconut cream from the top of the tins in a saucepan, bring to a rapid simmer over medium heat, stirring occasionally, and cook for 5–10 minutes, or until the mixture 'splits' (the oil starts to separate). Stir in 3 tablespoons of the curry paste, reduce the heat and simmer for 10 minutes, or until fragrant.

Stir in the remaining coconut cream, scallops and prawns, and cook for 5 minutes, or until tender. Add the fish sauce, palm sugar, makrut leaves and chilli, and cook for 1 minute. Stir in half the Thai basil and garnish with the remaining leaves.

Note: Krachai (bottled lesser galangal) is available from Asian food stores. It can be omitted from the paste if unavailable.

the perfect curry paste

Commercially produced curry pastes certainly have their place, but nothing will ever compete with a fresh, home-made batch — the benefits far outweighing the effort. Not only will your curry have better flavour but there is a certain amount of joy involved in selecting, sniffing and touching fresh, exotic ingredients then taking the time and care to finely grind them, releasing fresh and spicy aromas into your home. It is the aromas and flavours generated by the release of natural oils during the grinding process that makes a made-from-scratch curry, unique and irresistible. You can also keep excess curry paste in an airtight container in the refrigerator for one week, or in the freezer for up to two months.

If you follow the guidelines below in conjunction with individual curry recipes you will achieve great results every time. Firstly, any fresh produce required should be just that — fresh, as well as firm, crisp, unblemished and aromatic. Shrivelled up leafy herbs and chillies, dried up garlic, ginger and lemon grass or soft onions will result in an inferior product. To obtain the maximum flavour and aroma from your curry pastes, put fresh ingredients into the hollow of a mortar then pound and grind with a pestle until the mixture becomes pulpy then as smooth as possible. This can take some time but it is worth it, not only flavourwise but for ensuring your curry has a consistent texture.

Spices should be bought in small quantities and used up quickly as they deteriorate when exposed to air. Fresh whole spices contain more essential oils — and therefore flavour — than pre-ground or those that have been sitting in the cupboard for some time. Dry fry the spices in a frying pan over medium–high heat for 2–3 minutes, or until fragrant, to release the oils and make the spices more brittle for grinding. To grind the spices, allow them to cool then tip into a mortar and pound with a pestle until finely ground. The grinding releases the flavours and aromas and allows them to travel more evenly through the curry.

butter chicken . . . . serves 4–6

FOR MANY WESTERNERS, THIS FAMOUS DISH IS THEIR FIRST EXPERIENCE OF INDIAN FOOD. BASED ON TANDOORI CHICKEN, BUT WITHOUT THE TANDOOR, IT IS A RICH BLEND OF AROMATIC SPICES, BUTTER OR GHEE, YOGHURT AND TOMATO PASTE. WHEN DONE PROPERLY, IT IS SUMPTUOUS AND VELVETY, NOT MERELY CREAMY.

peanut oil	2 tablespoons
chicken thigh fillets	1 kg (2 lb 4 oz), quartered
butter or ghee	100 g (3 1/2 oz)
garam masala	3 teaspoons
sweet paprika	2 teaspoons
ground coriander	1 tablespoon
ginger	1 tablespoon finely chopped
ground cumin	3 teaspoons
garlic	2 cloves, crushed
chilli powder	1/4 teaspoon
cinnamon stick	1
cardamom pods	5, bruised
tomato paste (concentrated purée)	2 1/2 tablespoons
sugar	1 tablespoon
plain yoghurt	90 g (3 1/4 oz/1/3 cup)
cream (whipping)	185 ml (6 fl oz/3/4 cup)
lemon juice	1 tablespoon

Heat a frying pan or wok until very hot, add 1 tablespoon oil and swirl to coat. Add half the chicken thigh fillets and stir-fry for 4 minutes, or until browned. Remove from the pan. Add extra oil, as needed, and cook the remaining chicken, then remove.

Reduce the heat, add the butter to the pan or wok and melt. Add the garam masala, sweet paprika, coriander, ginger, cumin, garlic, chilli powder, cinnamon stick and cardamom pods, and stir-fry for 1 minute, or until fragrant. Return the chicken to the pan and mix in the spices so it is well coated.

Add the tomato paste and sugar, and simmer, stirring, for 15 minutes, or until the chicken is tender and the sauce has thickened. Add the yoghurt, cream and lemon juice and simmer for 5 minutes, or until the sauce has thickened slightly.

Stir-fry the spices in a frying pan or wok until fragrant.

Mix to coat the chicken well in the spice mixture.

Stir in the tomato paste and sugar and simmer.

musaman beef curry .... serves 4

THIS RICH, CREAMY CURRY IS A CLASSIC AMONG THAI CURRIES. ITS ORIGINS ARE UNCLEAR BUT TODAY IT IS MAINLY ASSOCIATED WITH THE SOUTHERN, MUSLIM AREAS OF THAILAND. COMPLEX WITH SWEET AND SOUR SPICES, IT IS UNUSUAL IN THAT IT ALSO INCORPORATES A STARCHY INGREDIENT SUCH AS POTATOES.

tamarind pulp	1 tablespoon
oil	2 tablespoons
lean stewing beef	750 g (1 lb 10 oz), cubed
coconut milk	500 ml (17 fl oz/2 cups)
cardamom pods	4, bruised
coconut cream	500 ml (17 fl oz/2 cups) (do not shake the tins)
musaman curry paste	2–3 tablespoons, ready-made or see recipe on page 17
baby onions	8
baby potatoes	8, cut in half if too large
fish sauce	2 tablespoons
palm sugar (jaggery)	2 tablespoons shaved
roasted ground peanuts	70 g (2½ oz/½ cup) unsalted
coriander (cilantro)	leaves, to serve

Put the tamarind pulp and 125 ml (4 fl oz/½ cup) boiling water in a bowl and set aside to cool. When cool, mash the pulp to dissolve in the water, then strain and reserve the liquid. Discard the pulp.

Heat the oil in a wok or a large saucepan and cook the beef in batches over high heat for 5 minutes, or until browned. Reduce the heat and add the coconut milk and cardamom, and simmer for 1 hour, or until the beef is tender. Remove the beef, strain and reserve the beef and cooking liquid.

Put the thick coconut cream from the top of the tins in a saucepan, bring to a rapid simmer over medium heat, stirring occasionally, and cook for 5–10 minutes, or until the mixture 'splits' (the oil starts to separate). Add the curry paste and cook for 5 minutes, or until it becomes aromatic.

Add the onions, potatoes, fish sauce, palm sugar, peanuts, beef, reserved cooking liquid and tamarind liquid, and simmer for 25–30 minutes. Garnish with fresh coriander leaves.

Pour boiling water onto the tamarind pulp to soften it.

Mash the pulp together with the water until as smooth as possible.

Strain the mashed pulp to obtain the tamarind liquid.

thai yellow vegetable curry . . . . serves 6

YELLOW CURRIES ARE FROM THAILAND'S SOUTHERN AREAS AND ARE CHARACTERIZED BY THEIR USE OF SPICES SUCH AS CORIANDER, CUMIN AND TURMERIC IN THE PASTE — THE TURMERIC PROVIDING THE LOVELY GOLDEN COLOURING. THEY ARE USUALLY OF MEDIUM STRENGTH, WET RATHER THAN DRY, AND DELICATELY SPICED.

yellow curry paste

green chillies	8
red Asian shallots	5, chopped
garlic	2 cloves, crushed
coriander (cilantro)	1 tablespoon finely chopped stem and root
lemon grass	1 stem, white part only, finely chopped
galangal	2 tablespoons finely chopped
ground coriander	1 teaspoon
ground cumin	1 teaspoon
ground turmeric	1/2 teaspoon
black peppercorns	1/2 teaspoon
lime juice	1 tablespoon

oil	3 tablespoons
onion	1, finely chopped
all-purpose potatoes	200 g (7 oz), diced
zucchini (courgette)	200 g (7 oz), diced
red capsicum (pepper)	150 g (5 1/2 oz), diced
beans	100 g (3 1/2 oz), trimmed, halved
bamboo shoots	50 g (1 3/4 oz), sliced
vegetable stock	250 ml (9 fl oz/1 cup)
coconut cream	400 ml (14 fl oz)
Thai basil	to serve

Put all the curry paste ingredients in a food processor, or in a mortar with a pestle, and process or pound to a smooth paste.

Heat the oil in a large saucepan, add the onion and cook over medium heat for 4–5 minutes, or until softened and just turning golden. Add 2 tablespoons of the made yellow curry paste and cook, stirring, for 2 minutes, or until fragrant.

Add all the vegetables and cook, stirring, over high heat for 2 minutes. Pour in the vegetable stock, reduce the heat to medium and cook, covered, for 15–20 minutes, or until the vegetables are tender. Cook, uncovered, over high heat for 5–10 minutes, or until the sauce has reduced slightly.

Stir in the coconut cream and season with salt to taste. Bring to the boil, stirring frequently, then reduce the heat and simmer for 5 minutes. Garnish with the Thai basil leaves.

earthy

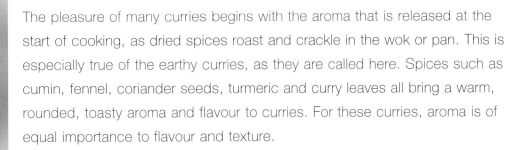

The pleasure of many curries begins with the aroma that is released at the start of cooking, as dried spices roast and crackle in the wok or pan. This is especially true of the earthy curries, as they are called here. Spices such as cumin, fennel, coriander seeds, turmeric and curry leaves all bring a warm, rounded, toasty aroma and flavour to curries. For these curries, aroma is of equal importance to flavour and texture.

Taking the time to grind and roast your own spices may seem like a luxury these days but it is one of the best, and most enjoyable, ways to learn about the different qualities of the spices that go into a curry. Coriander seeds, for example, have a sweet, heady aroma, suggestive of pine and pepper, while warm and bitter cumin is immediately distinctive. Fennel seeds have a subtle anise aroma and warm, sweet, intense flavour that mellows on roasting. Different again are potent cloves, with their sharp and woody flavours contributing to many curry powders, and versatile, pungent turmeric. Hidden within the unassuming dull brown skin of this root is a vibrantly coloured golden interior that, as a ground powder, is used in countless curries to balance and enhance the other flavours.

Many of these spices have been known for millennia — coriander is mentioned in ancient Sanskrit texts, and turmeric was included in an Assyrian manuscript dating back to 600 BC. The longevity of these spices is reflected in some of the recipes in this chapter. Both aromatic and slow-cooking rogan josh and the equally luxurious lamb dhansak from India have their origins in Persia, whose traditional cooking is renowned for its subtle and sophisticated use of spices. Also in this chapter is beef rendang, eaten throughout Indonesia and Malaysia. A classic of one-pot cooking, the meat is tender and the flavour welcoming. There are also a number of dishes from Sri Lanka, whose curry powders typically feature cardamom, cloves, cumin seeds, coriander and cinnamon, and are characterized by a dark, roasted flavour and aroma. Overall, the curries in this chapter share a depth of sensuous flavour and aroma that is not always anticipated — which makes cooking and eating them all the more enjoyable.

chicken and thai apple eggplant curry . . . . serves 4

THIS SAVOURY CURRY HAS LOTS OF FLAVOUR AND IS WELL BALANCED — NOT TOO HOT, SWEET OR SOUR. THAI APPLE EGGPLANTS (AUBERGINE) CAN BE A BIT OF AN ACQUIRED TASTE. WHEN FRESH, THEY ARE CRISP AND CLEAN AND ALMOST SWEET TASTING, BUT WHEN OLD AND MUSTY, BECOME QUITE BITTER.

curry paste

white peppercorns	1 teaspoon
dried shrimp	2 tablespoons
shrimp paste	1 teaspoon
coriander (cilantro)	2 tablespoons chopped root
lemon grass	3 stems, white part only, thinly sliced
garlic	3 cloves
ginger	1 tablespoon finely chopped
red chilli	1, chopped
makrut (kaffir lime) leaves	4
fish sauce	3 tablespoons
lime juice	3 tablespoons
ground turmeric	1 teaspoon
chicken thigh fillets	500 g (1 lb 2 oz)
Thai apple eggplant (aubergine)	250 g (9 oz)
coconut cream	400 ml (14 fl oz) (do not shake the tin)
palm sugar (jaggery)	2 tablespoons shaved
red capsicum (pepper)	1, sliced
water chestnuts	230 g (8 1/2 oz) tinned, sliced, drained
coriander (cilantro)	1 tablespoon chopped leaves
Thai basil	1 tablespoon chopped

Dry-fry the peppercorns, dried shrimp and the shrimp paste wrapped in some foil in a frying pan over medium–high heat for 2–3 minutes, or until fragrant. Allow to cool. Using a mortar with a pestle, or a spice grinder, crush or grind the peppercorns to a powder. Process the dried shrimp in a food processor until it becomes very finely shredded — forming a 'floss'.

Put the crushed peppercorns, shredded dried shrimp and the shrimp paste with the remaining curry paste ingredients in a food processor, or in a mortar with a pestle, and process or pound to a smooth paste.

Cut the chicken thigh fillets into 2.5 cm (1 in) cubes. Cut the eggplant into pieces of a similar size.

Put the thick coconut cream from the top of the tin in a saucepan, bring to a rapid simmer over medium heat, stirring occasionally, and cook for 5–10 minutes, or until the mixture 'splits' (the oil starts to separate). Add the curry paste and stir for 5–6 minutes, or until fragrant. Add the palm sugar and stir until dissolved.

Add the chicken, eggplant, capsicum, half the remaining coconut cream and the water chestnuts. Bring to the boil, cover and reduce to a simmer and cook for 15 minutes, or until the chicken is cooked and eggplant soft. Stir in the remaining coconut cream, coriander and basil.

Note: Thai apple eggplants are available from Asian food stores over summer and into early autumn.

Finely grind the peppercorns in a mortar or use a spice grinder.

Cut the eggplant into pieces similar in size to the chicken.

sri lankan pepper beef curry . . . . serves 6

SRI LANKA BOASTS A CUISINE THAT HAS BEEN INFLUENCED BY THE INDIANS, MALAYS, PORTUGUESE, DUTCH AND BRITISH. ITS CURRIES ARE MOSTLY COCONUT BASED, AND STRONG WITH SPICES. MANY, SUCH AS THIS ONE, ARE COOKED FOR HOURS, UNTIL THE THICK, FLAVOURSOME SAUCE CLINGS TO THE BY-NOW TENDER MAIN INGREDIENT.

coriander seeds	1 tablespoon
cumin seeds	2 teaspoons
fennel seeds	1 teaspoon
black peppercorns	1 tablespoon
oil	3 tablespoons
beef chuck	1 kg (2 lb 4 oz), diced
onions	2, finely diced
garlic	4 cloves, crushed
ginger	3 teaspoons finely grated
red chilli	1, seeded, finely chopped
curry leaves	8
lemon grass	1 stem, white part only, finely chopped
lemon juice	2 tablespoons
coconut milk	250 ml (9 fl oz/1 cup)
beef stock	250 ml (9 fl oz/1 cup)

Dry-fry the coriander seeds, cumin seeds, fennel seeds, and black peppercorns in a frying pan over medium–high heat for 2–3 minutes, or until fragrant. Allow to cool. Using a mortar with a pestle, or a spice grinder, crush or grind to a powder.

In a heavy-based saucepan, heat the oil over high heat, brown the beef in batches, and set aside. Reduce heat to medium, add the onion, garlic, ginger, chilli, curry leaves, and lemon grass, and cook for 5–6 minutes, or until softened. Add the ground spices and cook for a further 3 minutes.

Put the beef back into the pan, and stir well to coat in the spices. Add the lemon juice, coconut milk and beef stock and bring to the boil. Reduce heat to low, cover and cook for 2 1/2 hours, or until the beef is very tender and the sauce is reduced. While cooking, skim any oil that comes to the surface and discard.

Stir the spices constantly to release the aroma.

Brown the beef in batches to ensure you don't crowd the pan.

Cook the onion and spices until the onion is softened.

fish in yoghurt curry .... serves 4

THE CREAMY TEXTURE OF THIS DISH BELIES THE DEPTH OF FLAVOUR IT HAS FROM THE CUMIN, CORIANDER AND TURMERIC. THICK YOGHURT IS AN EXCELLENT WAY TO PROTECT THE FISH DURING COOKING AND ALSO ABSORBS SOME OF THE STING FROM THE CHILLIES. FOR BEST RESULTS USE A THICK, SET YOGHURT.

skinless, firm white fish fillets	1 kg (2 lb 4 oz)
oil	3 tablespoons
onion	1, chopped
ginger	2 tablespoons finely chopped
garlic	6 cloves, crushed
ground cumin	1 teaspoon
ground coriander	2 teaspoons
ground turmeric	1/4 teaspoon
garam masala	1 teaspoon
Greek-style yoghurt	185 g (6 1/2 oz/3/4 cup)
long green chillies	4, seeded, finely chopped
coriander (cilantro)	leaves, to serve

Cut each fish fillet into four pieces and thoroughly pat them dry. Heat the oil in a heavy-based frying pan over low heat and fry the onion until softened and lightly browned. Add the ginger, garlic and spices and stir for 2 minutes. Add the yoghurt and green chilli and bring to the boil, then cover and simmer for 10 minutes.

Slide in the pieces of fish and continue to simmer for 10–12 minutes, or until the fish flakes easily and is cooked through. Don't overcook or the fish will give off liquid and the sauce will split.

Garnish with coriander leaves and serve immediately. If you let the dish sit, the fish may give off liquid and make the sauce more runny.

Knobbly ginger 'hands' are familiar to most cooks today, but it can still be surprising to discover that the plant has been cultivated for millennia in China. Thought to be indigenous to northern India, ginger is used extensively in Chinese, Indian and Asian cooking for its sweet aroma and peppery, tangy flavour. It is featured in soups, curries and salads, and in relishes for its clean, digestive qualities. When buying, look for plump examples with pink-beige skin. The flesh inside should be moist and creamy-lemon. Ginger is also available dried, ground and pickled.

burmese chicken curry .... serves 6

NOT SURPRISINGLY FOR A COUNTRY BORDERED BY FIVE OTHER COUNTRIES, THE CUISINE OF BURMA (MYANMAR) SHOWS VARIOUS OUTSIDE INFLUENCES — IN PARTICULAR THAI, INDIAN AND CHINESE. BURMESE CURRIES ARE GENERALLY NOT AS SPICY AS INDIAN ONES, THOUGH THEY SHARE A LOVE OF AROMATIC FLAVOURS.

medium-spiced Indian curry powder	1 tablespoon
garam masala	1 teaspoon
cayenne pepper	1/2 teaspoon
sweet paprika	2 teaspoons
chicken	1.6 kg (3 lb 8 oz), cut into 8 pieces or 1.6 kg (3 lb 8 oz) mixed chicken pieces
onions	2, chopped
garlic	3 cloves, crushed
ginger	2 teaspoons grated
tomatoes	2, chopped
tomato paste (concentrated purée)	2 teaspoons
lemon grass	1 stem, white part only, thinly sliced
oil	3 tablespoons
chicken stock	500 ml (17 fl oz/2 cups)
sugar	1/2 teaspoon
fish sauce	1 tablespoon

Mix the curry powder, garam masala, cayenne pepper and paprika in a bowl. Rub this spice mix all over the chicken pieces and set aside.

Put the onions, garlic, ginger, tomatoes, tomato paste and lemon grass in a food processor, or in a mortar with a pestle, and process or pound to a smooth paste.

In a large heavy-based frying pan (that will fit the chicken pieces in a single layer), heat the oil over medium heat, add the chicken and brown all over, then remove from the pan. In the same frying pan, add the onion paste, and cook over low heat for 5–8 minutes stirring constantly. Put the chicken back into the pan, and turn to coat in the paste.

Add the chicken stock and sugar and bring to a simmer. Reduce heat to low, cover and cook for 1 1/4 hours, or until the chicken is very tender. While cooking, skim any oil that comes to the surface and discard. Stir in the fish sauce and serve.

Rub the spice mixture well into the chicken pieces.

Process or pound the paste ingredients until smooth.

beef rendang .... serves 6

IN THIS FESTIVE DISH OF INDONESIA AND MALAYSIA, BEEF IS COOKED UNTIL TENDER AND COATED IN A RICH, THICK SAUCE, THE WHOLE PERMEATED WITH THE WARM, COMPLEX AROMA AND FLAVOUR OF SPICES AND SEASONINGS. JUSTIFIABLY POPULAR, IT IS ALSO EASY TO MAKE, WITH EVERYTHING GOING INTO THE ONE POT.

beef chuck	1.5 kg (3 lb 5 oz)
onions	2, roughly chopped
garlic	2 cloves, crushed
coconut milk	400 ml (14 fl oz)
ground coriander	2 teaspoons
ground fennel	1/2 teaspoon
ground cumin	2 teaspoons
ground cloves	1/4 teaspoon
red chillies	4–6, chopped
lemon juice	1 tablespoon
lemon grass	1 stem, white part only, cut lengthways
palm sugar (jaggery)	2 teaspoons shaved

Trim the meat of any excess fat or sinew and cut into 3 cm (1 1/4 in) cubes. Put the onion and garlic in a food processor, or in a mortar with a pestle, and process or pound to a smooth paste.

Put the coconut milk in a large saucepan and bring to the boil, then reduce the heat to medium and cook, stirring occasionally, for 15 minutes, or until the milk has reduced by half and the oil has separated. Do not allow the milk to brown.

Add the coriander, fennel, cumin and cloves to the pan, and stir for 1 minute. Add the meat and cook for 2 minutes, or until it changes colour. Add the onion mixture, chilli, lemon juice, lemon grass and sugar. Cook, covered, over medium heat for 2 hours, or until the liquid has reduced and the mixture has thickened. Stir frequently to prevent it sticking to the bottom of the pan.

Uncover and continue cooking until the oil from the coconut milk begins to emerge again, letting the curry develop colour and flavour. Be careful that it does not burn. The curry is cooked when it is brown and dry.

Simmer the coconut milk until the oil 'splits' — it separates.

Add the spices to the coconut milk and cook until fragrant.

lamb dhansak..serves 6

THIS SUMPTUOUS CURRY COMES FROM THE PARSEES OF WEST INDIA, WHO EMIGRATED THERE FROM IRAN IN THE SEVENTH CENTURY. IT IS STRIKING FOR THE NUMBER OF DIFFERENT LENTILS USED, AS WELL AS VEGETABLES SUCH AS ENGLISH SPINACH, PUMPKIN AND EGGPLANT (AUBERGINE), VARIOUS SPICES AND TENDER LAMB.

yellow lentils	100 g (3¹/2 oz/³/4 cup)
dried yellow mung beans	2 teaspoons
dried chickpeas	2 tablespoons
red lentils	3 tablespoons
eggplant (aubergine)	1, unpeeled
pumpkin (winter squash)	150 g (5¹/2 oz), unpeeled
ghee or oil	2 tablespoons
onion	1, finely chopped
garlic	3 cloves, crushed
ginger	1 tablespoon grated
boneless leg or shoulder of lamb	1 kg (2 lb 4 oz), cut into 3 cm (1¹/4 in) cubes
cinnamon stick	1
cardamom pods	5, bruised
cloves	3
ground coriander	1 tablespoon
ground turmeric	1 teaspoon
chilli powder	1 teaspoon, or to taste
amaranth or English spinach leaves	150 g (5¹/2 oz), cut into 5 cm (2 in) lengths
tomatoes	2, halved
long green chillies	2, split lengthways, seeded
lime juice	3 tablespoons

Soak the yellow lentils, yellow mung beans and chickpeas in water for about 2 hours, then drain well.

Put all four types of pulse in a saucepan, add 1 litre (35 fl oz/ 4 cups) water, cover and bring to the boil. Uncover and simmer for 15 minutes, skimming off any scum that forms on the surface, and stirring occasionally to make sure all the pulses are cooking at the same rate and are soft. Drain the pulses and lightly mash to a similar texture.

Cook the eggplant and pumpkin in boiling water for 10–15 minutes, or until soft. Scoop out the pumpkin flesh and cut it into pieces. Peel the eggplant carefully (it may be very pulpy) and cut the flesh into small pieces.

Heat the ghee or oil in a casserole dish or karahi (see note below) and fry the onion, garlic and ginger for 5 minutes, or until lightly brown and softened. Add the lamb and brown for 10 minutes, or until aromatic. Add the cinnamon, cardamom pods, cloves, coriander, turmeric and chilli powder and fry for 5 minutes to allow the flavours to develop. Add 170 ml (5¹/2 fl oz/²/3 cup) water, cover and simmer for 40 minutes, or until the lamb is tender.

Add the mashed lentils and all the cooked and raw vegetables to the pan. Add the lime juice and simmer for 15 minutes (if the sauce is too thick, add a little water). Stir well, then check the seasoning. The dhansak should be flavoursome, aromatic, tart and spicy.

Note: A karahi is a deep, wok-shaped cooking dish used in Indian and Balti cooking. It lends itself perfectly to one-pot meals and can be taken straight from the stove to the table for serving.

spicy prawns .... serves 4–6

TURMERIC IS AT THE HEART OF SO MANY CURRIES. IT IMPARTS NOT JUST COLOUR, BUT ALSO A SUBTLE AROMA AND EARTHY, SLIGHTLY BITTER FLAVOUR. USING GROUND TURMERIC IS EASY AND CONVENIENT BUT BUY SOME FRESH TURMERIC ROOT IF YOU SEE IT. IT LOOKS SIMILAR TO OLD GINGER, BUT INSIDE IT IS WONDERFULLY GOLDEN.

raw prawns (shrimp)	1 kg (2 lb 4 oz), peeled, deveined, tails intact (reserve shells and heads)
ground turmeric	1 teaspoon
oil	3 tablespoons
onions	2, finely chopped
garlic	4–6 cloves, crushed
green chillies	1–2, seeded, chopped
ground cumin	2 teaspoons
ground coriander	2 teaspoons
paprika	1 teaspoon
plain yoghurt	90 g (3 1/4 oz/1/3 cup)
thickened (whipping) cream	80 ml (2 1/2 fl oz/1/3 cup)
coriander (cilantro)	1 large handful leaves, chopped

Bring 1 litre (35 fl oz/4 cups) water to the boil in a saucepan. Add the reserved prawn shells and heads, reduce the heat and simmer for 2 minutes. Skim any scum that forms on the surface during cooking. Strain, discard the shells and heads and return the liquid to the pan. You will need about 750 ml (26 fl oz/3 cups) liquid (make up with water if necessary). Add the turmeric and peeled prawns, and cook for 1 minute, or until the prawns just turn pink, then remove the prawns. Reserve the stock.

Heat the oil in a large saucepan. Add the onion and cook over a medium heat, stirring, for 8 minutes, or until lightly golden brown. Add the garlic and chilli, and cook for 1–2 minutes, then add the cumin, coriander and paprika, and cook, stirring, for 1–2 minutes, or until fragrant.

Gradually add the reserved stock, bring to the boil and cook, stirring occasionally, for 30–35 minutes, or until the mixture has reduced by half and thickened. Remove from the heat and stir in the yoghurt. Add the prawns and stir over low heat for 2–3 minutes, or until the prawns are warmed through. Do not boil. Stir in the cream and coriander leaves. Cover and leave to stand for 15 minutes to allow the flavours to infuse. Reheat gently and serve.

Simmer the prawn shells and heads, skimming the surface.

Poach the prawns in the stock until just pink and curled.

Gradually add the reserved prawn stock to the saucepan.

beef and mustard seed curry .... serves 6

THIS COMFORTING CURRY LOOKS AFTER ITSELF ONCE THE INITIAL FRYING OF THE SPICES IS DONE. STAY CLOSE WHILE COOKING THE SPICES TO ENSURE THAT THEY DO NOT BURN. THE MUSTARD SEEDS, IN PARTICULAR, GIVE THIS DISH A DISTINCTIVE FLAVOUR — HEATING THEM UNTIL THEY POP BRINGS OUT THEIR PLEASANT NUTTY TASTE.

oil	3 tablespoons
brown mustard seeds	2 tablespoons
dried red chillies	4
yellow split peas	1 tablespoon
French shallots	200 g (7 oz), finely sliced
garlic	8 cloves, crushed
ginger	1 tablespoons finely grated
curry leaves	15
ground turmeric	1/2 teaspoon
tomatoes	420 g (15 oz) tinned, chopped
beef chuck	1 kg (2 lb 4 oz), diced
beef stock	435 ml (15 1/4 fl oz/1 3/4 cups)

Put the oil in a heavy-based saucepan over medium heat, add the mustard seeds, chillies and split peas. As soon as the mustard seeds start to pop, add the shallots, garlic, ginger, curry leaves and turmeric. Cook for 5 minutes, then add the tomatoes, beef and stock.

Bring to the boil then reduce to a simmer, cover and cook for 2 hours, or until the beef is very tender and the sauce reduced. While cooking, skim any oil that comes to the surface and discard.

Shiny, dark green curry leaves are from a tropical evergreen tree native to Sri Lanka and India. The tree is a relative of the lemon tree, and shares its lingering citrusy, slightly spicy aroma. Fresh curry leaves are used widely in southern Indian, Sri Lankan and Malay cooking. When added whole to dishes, the leaves are first cooked in oil to extract their aroma and distinct flavour, then discarded at the end and not eaten. They are also used as a garnish. Fresh leaves should be kept in the refrigerator. If buying dried leaves, choose ones that have retained their green colour.

three ways with coconut

THE COCONUT PALM GROWS ALL OVER ASIA AND SUCH IS THE IMPORTANCE OF THE FRUIT THAT IT IS KNOWN AS SHRIFAL, OR 'FRUIT OF LUSTRE', IN PARTS OF INDIA. COUNTLESS CURRIES ARE BASED ON COCONUT MILK OR CREAM, WHICH ARE ALSO USED IN SOUPS, SALADS AND PASTRIES. THE DESICCATED FLESH IS USED IN GARNISHES, CHUTNEYS, RAITAS AND DESSERTS. WHEN SERVED ALONGSIDE OR AFTER A SPICY CURRY, COCONUT SIDES AND DRINKS CAN EITHER SOOTHE AND REFRESH PALATES, OR ADD A LITTLE EXTRA SPICINESS TO THE MAIN EVENT.

coconut and coriander chutney

Put 90 g (3^1/4 oz) roughly chopped coriander (cilantro), including the roots, 25 g (1 oz/^{1}/4 cup) desiccated coconut, 1 tablespoon soft brown sugar, 1 tablespoon grated ginger, 1 chopped small onion, 2 tablespoons lemon juice, 1–2 seeded green chillies and 1 teaspoon salt in a food processor and process for 1 minute, or until finely chopped. Refrigerate until ready to serve. There are numerous variations, depending on region and tastes. Try substituting 1 handful of roughly chopped mint leaves for the coriander in this recipe, or add 5 roughly chopped spring onions (scallions), including the green part, instead of the onion. If you prefer more fire in your chutney, do not remove the seeds from the chillies. Serves 4.

coconut and pineapple cooler

Peel and chop 2 pineapples and juice through a juice extractor. Transfer the pineapple juice to a large jug and stir through 500 ml (17 fl oz/2 cups) of coconut milk. Pour 250 ml (9 fl oz/1 cup) of the mixture into 16 holes of an ice-cube tray and freeze. Chill the remaining mixture. When the ice cubes have frozen, pour the juice mixture into 4 glasses, add the ice cubes and garnish with mint and pineapple leaves. Serves 4.

fresh coconut chutney

Soak 1 teaspoon chana dal (gram lentils) and 1 teaspoon urad dal (black lentils) in cold water for 2 hours, then drain well. Put the grated flesh from half a fresh coconut, 2 seeded and chopped green chillies and ^{1}/2 teaspoon salt in a food processor, or in a mortar with a pestle, and process or pound to a smooth paste. Heat 1 tablespoon oil in a small saucepan and add 1 teaspoon black mustard seeds and the dals, then cover and shake the pan until they pop. Add 5 curry leaves and fry for 1 minute, or until the dal browns. Add these ingredients to the coconut with 1 teaspoon tamarind purée and mix well. Serves 4.

onion bhaji curry
.... serves 4

THESE BHAJIS GET THEIR DISTINCTIVE TASTE AND COLOUR FROM NUTTY-TASTING, YELLOW BESAN FLOUR AND TURMERIC. THEY ALSO CONTAIN ASAFOETIDA, A DRIED RESIN WHOSE PUNGENT AROMA HAS EARNED IT THE NAME 'DEVIL'S DUNG'. IT IS WIDELY USED IN INDIA, TO FLAVOUR A DISH AND FOR ITS MEDICINAL PROPERTIES.

oil	2 tablespoons
ginger	1 teaspoon grated
garlic	2 cloves, crushed
tomatoes	425 g (15 oz) tinned, crushed
ground turmeric	1/4 teaspoon
chilli powder	1/2 teaspoon
ground cumin	1 1/2 teaspoons
ground coriander	1 teaspoon
garam masala	1 1/2 tablespoons
cream (whipping)	250 ml (9 fl oz/1 cup)
coriander (cilantro)	chopped leaves, to serve

bhajis

besan (chickpea flour)	125 g (4 1/2 oz/1 1/4 cups)
ground turmeric	1/4 teaspoon
chilli powder	1/2 teaspoon
asafoetida	1/4 teaspoon
onion	1, thinly sliced
oil	for deep-frying

Heat the oil in a frying pan, add the ginger and garlic, and cook for 2 minutes, or until fragrant. Add the tomato, turmeric, chilli powder, cumin, coriander and 250 ml (9 fl oz/1 cup) water. Bring to the boil, then reduce the heat and simmer for 5 minutes, or until thickened slightly. Add the garam masala, stir in the cream and simmer for 1–2 minutes. Remove from heat.

To make the bhajis, combine the besan, turmeric, chilli powder and asafoetida with 125 ml (4 fl oz/1/2 cup) water, and salt to taste. Whisk to make a smooth batter, then stir in the onion.

Fill a deep heavy-based saucepan one-third full of oil and heat to 160°C (315°F), or until a cube of bread dropped into the oil browns in 30 seconds. Add spoonfuls of the onion mixture in batches and cook for 1–2 minutes, or until golden brown all over, then drain on paper towel. Pour the sauce over the bhajis and garnish with the coriander leaves.

Coat the sliced onion well in the smooth besan batter.

Deep-fry spoonfuls of the bhaji mixture until crisp and golden.

malaysian chicken curry .... serves 4-6

MALAYSIAN CUISINE IS AN EXCITING MIX OF OUTSIDE INFLUENCES — FROM THAI TO EUROPEAN — WITH ITS OWN, OFTEN HIGHLY REGIONAL, DISTINCTIVE CHARACTERISTICS. CURRIES OFTEN DRAW ON THE SPICES OF INDIA AND THE SEASONINGS OF THAI CURRIES, BLENDING THEM WITH SHRIMP PASTE, COCONUT MILK, CHILLIES AND CANDLENUTS.

dried shrimp	3 teaspoons
oil	80 ml (2½ fl oz/⅓ cup)
red chillies	6–8, seeded, finely chopped
garlic	4 cloves, crushed
lemon grass	3 stems, white part only, finely chopped
ground turmeric	2 teaspoons
candlenuts	10
onions	2 large, chopped
coconut milk	250 ml (9 fl oz/1 cup)
whole chicken	1.5 kg (3 lb 5 oz), cut into 8 pieces
coconut cream	125 ml (4 fl oz/½ cup)
lime juice	2 tablespoons

Put the shrimp in a frying pan and dry-fry over low heat, shaking the pan regularly, for 3 minutes, or until the shrimp are dark orange and are giving off a strong aroma. Allow to cool.

Put the shrimp, half the oil, chilli, garlic, lemon grass, turmeric and candlenuts in a food processor, or in a mortar with a pestle, and process or pound to a smooth paste.

Heat the remaining oil in a wok or frying pan, add the onion and ¼ teaspoon salt, and cook, stirring regularly, over low–medium heat for 8 minutes, or until golden. Add the spice paste and stir for 5 minutes. If the mixture begins to stick to the bottom of the pan, add 2 tablespoons coconut milk. It is important to cook the mixture thoroughly as this develops the flavours.

Add the chicken to the wok or pan and cook, stirring, for 5 minutes, or until it begins to brown. Stir in the remaining coconut milk and 250 ml (9 fl oz/1 cup) water, and bring to the boil. Reduce the heat and simmer for 50 minutes, or until the chicken is cooked and the sauce has thickened slightly. Add the coconut cream and bring the mixture back to the boil, stirring constantly. Add the lime juice and serve immediately.

Dry-fry the shrimp until dark orange and aromatic.

If using a food processor, scrape down the sides of the bowl.

spinach koftas in yoghurt sauce .... serves 4

GUJARATI DISHES SUCH AS THIS ARE UNIQUE IN INDIA IN THAT THEY ARE NEARLY ALWAYS VEGETARIAN. CURRIES ARE TYPICALLY MILD — THOUGH SOUTHERN GUJARATI CUISINE HAS A PENCHANT FOR GREEN CHILLIES — AND RELY ON FRESH VEGETABLES, YOGHURT, AND ACCOMPANYING PICKLES AND CHUTNEYS FOR EXTRA SPICE.

yoghurt sauce

plain yoghurt	375 g (13 oz/1½ cups)
besan (chickpea flour)	35 g (1¼ oz/⅓ cup)
oil	1 tablespoon
black mustard seeds	2 teaspoons
fenugreek seeds	1 teaspoon
curry leaves	6
onion	1 large, finely chopped
garlic	3 cloves, crushed
ground turmeric	1 teaspoon
chilli powder	½ teaspoon

koftas

English spinach	450 g (1 lb/1 bunch), leaves picked off the stems
besan (chickpea flour)	170 g (6 oz/1½ cups)
red onion	1, finely chopped
tomato	1 ripe, finely diced
garlic	2 cloves, crushed
ground cumin	1 teaspoon
coriander (cilantro)	2 tablespoons chopped leaves
oil	for deep-frying
coriander (cilantro)	leaves, to serve

To make the yoghurt sauce whisk the yoghurt, besan and 750 ml (26 fl oz/3 cups) water in a bowl, to a smooth paste. Heat the oil in a heavy-based saucepan or deep frying pan over low heat.

Add the mustard and fenugreek seeds and the curry leaves, cover and allow the seeds to pop for 1 minute. Add the onion and cook for 5 minutes, or until soft and starting to brown.

Add the garlic and stir for 1 minute, or until soft. Add the turmeric and chilli powder and stir for 30 seconds. Add the yoghurt mixture, bring to the boil and simmer over low heat for 10 minutes.

To make the spinach koftas, blanch the spinach in boiling water for 1 minute and refresh in cold water. Drain, squeeze out any extra water by putting the spinach in a colander and pressing it against the sides with a spoon. Finely chop the spinach. Combine with the remaining kofta ingredients and up to 3 tablespoons water, a little at a time, adding enough to make the mixture soft but not sloppy. If it becomes too sloppy, add more besan. Shape the mixture into balls by rolling it in dampened hands, using about 1 tablespoon of mixture for each. This should make 12 koftas.

Fill a heavy-based saucepan one-third full with oil and heat to 180°C (350°F), or until a cube of bread browns in 15 seconds. Lower the koftas into the oil in batches and fry until golden and crisp. Don't overcrowd the pan. Remove the koftas as they cook, shake off any excess oil and add them to the yoghurt sauce. Gently reheat the yoghurt sauce, garnish with coriander leaves and serve.

dal

IN INDIA, DAL REFERS TO BOTH THE DRIED PULSE AND THE FINISHED DISH. IN THIS RECIPE, LENTILS ARE USED, BUT CHICKPEAS AND OTHER BEANS AND PEAS ARE ALSO POPULAR. TO BOLSTER THE SIMPLE FLAVOUR OF THE LENTILS, SPICES SUCH AS CUMIN AND ASAFOETIDA ARE FRIED IN GHEE, RELEASING THEIR EARTHY AROMAS.

red lentils	200 g (7 oz/³/4 cup)
ginger	3 thick slices
ground turmeric	1/2 teaspoon
ghee or oil	1 tablespoon
garlic	2 cloves, crushed
onion	1, finely chopped
yellow mustard seeds	1/2 teaspoon
asafoetida	pinch, optional
cumin seeds	1 teaspoon
ground coriander	1 teaspoon
green chillies	2, halved lengthways
lemon juice	2 tablespoons

Put the lentils and 750 ml (26 fl oz/3 cups) water in a saucepan, and bring to the boil. Reduce the heat, add the ginger and turmeric, and simmer, covered, for 20 minutes, or until the lentils are tender. Stir occasionally to prevent the lentils sticking to the pan. Remove the ginger and season the lentil mixture with salt.

Heat the ghee or oil in a frying pan, add the garlic, onion and mustard seeds, and cook over medium heat for 5 minutes, or until the onion is golden. Add the asafoetida, cumin seeds, ground coriander and chilli, and cook for 2 minutes.

Add the onion mixture to the lentils and stir gently to combine. Add 125 ml (4 fl oz/1/2 cup) water, reduce the heat to low and cook for 5 minutes. Stir in the lemon juice and serve.

Add the ginger slices and turmeric to the lentils and simmer.

Cook the onion, mustard seeds and garlic until the onion is golden.

Stir the onion mixture gently through the lentil mixture.

jungle curry prawns .... serves 6

BE WARNED: JUNGLE CURRIES ARE GENERALLY HOT CURRIES! TRADITIONALLY, THERE IS NO COCONUT TO ABSORB THE HEAT OF THE CHILLIES. HOWEVER, THEY USUALLY ALSO FEATURE PLENTY OF FRESH SPICES AND VEGETABLES, AS IS THE CASE HERE. THE FINAL FLAVOUR IS AROMATIC, HOT AND SALTY, BUT NOT SCORCHING.

jungle curry paste

dried red chillies	10–12
white pepper	1 teaspoon
red Asian shallots	4
garlic	4 cloves
lemon grass	1 stem, white part only, chopped
galangal	1 tablespoon finely chopped
coriander (cilantro)	2 roots
ginger	1 tablespoon finely chopped
shrimp paste	1 tablespoon dry roasted
peanut oil	1 tablespoon
garlic	1 clove, crushed
fish sauce	1 tablespoon
ground candlenuts	30 g (1 oz/¼ cup)
fish stock	300 ml (10½ fl oz)
whisky	1 tablespoon
makrut (kaffir lime) leaves	3, torn
raw prawns (shrimp)	600 g (1 lb 5 oz) peeled, deveined, tails intact
carrot	1 small, quartered lengthways, sliced thinly on the diagonal
snake (yard-long) beans	150 g (5½ oz), cut into 2 cm (¾ in) lengths
bamboo shoots	50 g (1¾ oz/¼ cup)
Thai basil	to serve

Soak the chillies in boiling water for 5 minutes, or until soft. Remove the stem and seeds, then chop. Put the chillies and the remaining curry paste ingredients in a food processor, or in a mortar with a pestle, and process or pound to a smooth paste. Add a little water if it is too thick.

Heat a wok over medium heat, add the oil and swirl to coat. Add the garlic and 3 tablespoons of the curry paste and cook, stirring, for 5 minutes. Add the fish sauce, ground candlenuts, fish stock, whisky, makrut leaves, prawns, carrot, beans and bamboo shoots. Bring to the boil, then reduce the heat and simmer for 5 minutes, or until the prawns and vegetables are cooked. Top with Thai basil and serve.

sri lankan fried pork curry.............................serves 6

THIS CURRY IS INTERESTING FOR THE NUMBER OF FLAVOURINGS NOT OFTEN SEEN IN WESTERN DISHES. FENUGREEK SEEDS ARE SMALL, HARD AND OCHRE-COLOURED. THEY ARE POWERFULLY SCENTED AND HAVE A BITTER TASTE, THOUGH THIS SOFTENS ON COOKING.

oil	80 ml (2¹/₂ fl oz/¹/₃ cup)
boned pork shoulder	1.25 kg (2 lb 12 oz), cut into 3 cm (1¹/₄ in) cubes
red onion	1 large, finely chopped
garlic	3–4 cloves, crushed
ginger	1 tablespoon grated
curry leaves	10
fenugreek seeds	¹/₂ teaspoon
chilli powder	¹/₂ teaspoon
cardamom pods	6, bruised
Sri Lankan curry powder	2¹/₂ tablespoons
white vinegar	1 tablespoon
tamarind concentrate	3 tablespoons
coconut cream	270 ml (9¹/₂ fl oz)

Heat half the oil in a large saucepan over high heat, add the meat and cook in batches for 6 minutes, or until well browned. Remove from the pan. Heat the remaining oil, add the onion and cook over medium heat for 5 minutes, or until lightly browned. Add the garlic and ginger, and cook for 2 minutes. Stir in the curry leaves, spices and curry powder, and cook for 2 minutes, or until fragrant. Stir in the vinegar and 1 teaspoon salt.

Return the browned meat to the pan, add the tamarind concentrate and 310 ml (10³/₄ fl oz/1¹/₄ cups) water and simmer, covered, stirring occasionally, for 40–50 minutes, or until the meat is tender. Stir in the coconut cream and simmer, uncovered, for 15 minutes, or until the sauce has reduced and thickened a little. Serve immediately.

The tropical tamarind tree is prized for its fruit pods, each containing a sticky, fleshy acidic pulp wrapped around small, shiny, dark-brown seeds. The tree is indigenous to east Africa but it flourishes wild in India where the pulp is greatly appreciated for its refreshing sweet–sour taste and fruity aroma. Across tropical Asia it serves as an excellent souring agent, and is used in soups, curries, chutneys, drinks and sweetmeats. In the West, its main use is in Worcestershire sauce. Tamarind is sold as a concentrated paste in jars, or in blocks or cakes that still contain the seeds. Store both in the refrigerator for up to 1 year.

rogan josh . . . . serves 6

THIS CLASSIC, SUPERBLY AROMATIC, SLOW-COOKING CURRY ORIGINATED IN PERSIA, AND TRAVELLED TO KASHMIR, IN INDIA'S FAR NORTH, UNDER THE MOGHUL EMPIRE. IN KASHMIR IT WAS ADAPTED AND PERFECTED, INCORPORATING THE LOCAL CHILLIES, SAFFRON AND CARDAMOM.

garlic	8 cloves, crushed
ginger	3 teaspoons grated
ground cumin	2 teaspoons
chilli powder	1 teaspoon
paprika	2 teaspoons
ground coriander	2 teaspoons
boneless leg or shoulder of lamb	1 kg (2 lb 4 oz), cut into 3 cm (1¼ in) cubes
ghee or oil	3 tablespoons
onion	1, finely chopped
cardamom pods	6, bruised
cloves	4
Indian bay (cassia) leaves	2
cinnamon stick	1
Greek-style yoghurt	185 g (6½ oz/¾ cup)
saffron	4 threads, mixed with 2 tablespoons milk
garam masala	¼ teaspoon

Mix the garlic, ginger, cumin, chilli powder, paprika and coriander in a large bowl. Add the meat and stir thoroughly to coat the meat cubes well. Cover and marinate for at least 2 hours, or overnight, in the refrigerator.

Heat the ghee or oil in a flameproof casserole dish or karahi over low heat. Add the onion and cook for about 10 minutes, or until the onion is lightly browned. Remove from the dish.

Add the cardamom pods, cloves, bay leaves and cinnamon to the dish and fry for 1 minute. Increase the heat to high, add the meat and onion, then mix well and fry for 2 minutes. Stir well, then reduce the heat to low, cover and cook for 15 minutes. Uncover and fry for another 3–5 minutes, or until the meat is quite dry. Add 100 ml (3½ fl oz) water, cover and cook for 5–7 minutes, until the water has evaporated and the oil separates out and floats on the surface. Fry the meat for another 1–2 minutes, then add 250 ml (9 fl oz/1 cup) water. Cover and cook for 40–50 minutes, gently simmering until the meat is tender. The liquid will reduce quite a bit.

Stir in the yoghurt when the meat is almost tender, taking care not to allow the meat to catch on the base of the dish. Add the saffron and milk. Stir the mixture a few times to mix in the saffron. Season with salt to taste. Remove from the heat and sprinkle with the garam masala.

Coat the meat well in the mixed spices and leave to marinate.

Cook the onion until lightly browned and remove from pan.

Dry-fry the spices for 1 minute, or until they become aromatic.

sri lankan eggplant curry . . . . serves 6

THERE ARE MANY SIMILARITIES BETWEEN INDIAN AND SRI LANKAN COOKING, BUT IT WOULD BE WRONG TO THINK THEY ARE INTERCHANGEABLE. CRUCIALLY, THEIR CURRY POWDERS DIFFER. SRI LANKAN CURRY POWDER IS MADE BY ROASTING SPICES SUCH AS CUMIN, FENNEL AND CORIANDER AND HAS A DARK, INTENSE FLAVOUR.

ground turmeric	1 teaspoon
slender eggplants (aubergines)	12, cut into 4 cm (1½ in) rounds
oil	for deep-frying, plus 2 tablespoons, extra
onions	2, finely chopped
Sri Lankan curry powder	2 tablespoons
garlic	2 cloves, crushed
curry leaves	8, roughly chopped, plus extra whole leaves for garnish
chilli powder	½ teaspoon
coconut cream	250 ml (9 fl oz/1 cup)

Mix half the ground turmeric with 1 teaspoon salt and rub into the eggplant, ensuring the cut surfaces are well coated. Put in a colander and leave for 1 hour. Rinse well and put on crumpled paper towel to remove any excess moisture.

Fill a deep heavy-based saucepan one-third full of oil and heat to 180°C (350°F), or until a cube of bread dropped into the oil browns in 15 seconds. Cook the eggplant in batches for 1 minute, or until golden brown. Drain on crumpled paper towel.

Heat the extra oil in a large saucepan, add the onion and cook over medium heat for 5 minutes, or until browned. Add the curry powder, garlic, curry leaves, chilli powder, eggplant and remaining turmeric to the pan, and cook for 2 minutes. Stir in the coconut cream and 250 ml (9 fl oz/1 cup) water, and season with salt to taste. Reduce the heat and simmer over low heat for 3 minutes, or until the eggplant is fully cooked and the sauce has thickened slightly. Garnish with extra curry leaves.

Rub the ground turmeric and salt into the eggplants' cut surfaces.

Fry the eggplant in a deep saucepan until golden and tender.

curried squid . . . . serves 4

THIS QUICK AND SIMPLE CURRY PACKS QUITE A FLAVOUR PUNCH. IT FEATURES THE ROUND, EARTHY FLAVOURS OF CUMIN AND TURMERIC, ALONGSIDE THE FRESH, SHARPER FLAVOURS OF CHILLI, GINGER AND LIME JUICE. VERSIONS OF THIS DISH ARE EATEN THROUGHOUT TROPICAL THAILAND, SINGAPORE AND MALAYSIA.

squid	1 kg (2 lb 4 oz)
cumin seeds	1 teaspoon
coriander seeds	1 teaspoon
chilli powder	1 teaspoon
ground turmeric	1/2 teaspoon
oil	2 tablespoons
onion	1, finely chopped
curry leaves	10, plus extra for garnish
fenugreek seeds	1/2 teaspoon
garlic	4 cloves, crushed
ginger	7 cm (2³/4 in) piece, grated
coconut cream	100 ml (3¹/2 fl oz)
lime juice	3 tablespoons

Pull the squid heads and tentacles out of their bodies, along with any innards, and discard. Peel off the skins. Rinse the bodies well, pulling out the clear quills, then cut the bodies into 2.5 cm (1 in) rings.

Dry-fry the cumin and coriander seeds in a frying pan over medium–high heat for 2–3 minutes, or until fragrant. Allow to cool. Using a mortar with a pestle, or a spice grinder, crush or grind to a powder. Mix the ground cumin and coriander with the chilli powder and ground turmeric. Add the squid and mix well.

In a heavy-based frying pan, heat the oil and fry the onion until lightly browned. Add the curry leaves, fenugreek, garlic, ginger and coconut cream. Bring slowly to the boil. Add the squid, then stir well. Simmer for 2–3 minutes, or until cooked and tender. Stir in the lime juice, season and serve garnished with curry leaves.

Wonderfully tangy and aromatic, lime are native to the tropics (possibly originating in Malaysia), where they are widely used in cooking. They are valued as a souring agent and are added to innumerable curries and stews and are particularly good in dipping sauces, chutneys and pickles, some of which can be quite sharp. It is not difficult to make your own lime pickles, but ready-made pickled limes are easily bought from Asian food stores. To get the maximum flavour impact from fresh limes, squeeze them only as needed — for this reason, too, the juice is generally added to a dish only at the end of cooking.

hot and sour

It has been said that chillies should be treated with respect, and most of us would agree with that. When scanning the ingredient lists of some of these curries, chillies seem to jump out, regardless of how many other ingredients surround them. Some of us relish the challenge of eating a hot curry; others would prefer to go hungry. But chillies need not — and generally should not — scorch. Rather, they should enhance the overall flavour and fragrance of a dish, with specific chillies being used for their different properties.

Having said that, there are certain curries where no other description besides 'fiery' will do. The jungle curries of Thailand, for example, some of Goa's seafood curries and many Malaysian and Balinese curries fall into this category. Chillies were introduced to Southeast Asia and India in the sixteenth century by traders and spicy dishes can reflect an area's mixed heritage. Goa's notoriously hot vindaloo curry began life as a vinegar and pork dish of the Portuguese, and the Nonya cooking of Malaysia, a mix of indigenous and Chinese cooking, is famous for its hot, tangy and aromatic curries.

If venturing into this taste arena for the first time, just remember that the active agent in chillies, capsaicin, is found mostly in the ribs and seeds of chillies. So, seeding a chilli is a fail-safe way of reducing heat levels. Otherwise, use less than the recipe specifies — you can always add more. As a general guide, the smaller the chilli, the hotter it will be. As well, have plain rice, yoghurt and chilled beer on standby when eating chilli-based dishes.

Chillies are not the only ingredient adding heat to a curry. Mustard seeds and peppercorns can also be extremely potent. But, as with chillies, searing heat is generally not the aim — both of these spices offer a warm, biting flavour and aroma that blend well with other fresh and dried spices and herbs. In particular, hot curries invite the use of sour flavours such as tamarind, tart vinegar and yoghurt and crisp, clean lime juice and lemon grass. The combination of hot and sour is a particularly happy one, with the sour elements adding an extra layer of flavour and fragrance to a hot dish. Sour ingredients also include a number of vegetables — such as bitter melon and Thai apple eggplants (aubergines) — that add textural interest. Even further complexity is added with the use of rich, creamy coconut milk. As with all curries, balance is the key.

pork vindaloo .... serves 4

THE PORTUGUESE FIRST INTRODUCED THIS PORK, GARLIC AND VINEGAR STEW TO GOA. THE LOCALS ADOPTED IT BUT, FINDING IT LACKING SLIGHTLY IN FLAVOUR, PROCEEDED TO ADAPT IT, ADDING SPICES, EXTRA GARLIC AND A HEFTY QUANTITY OF CHILLIES. THE RESULT IS *VINDALOO*, FAMED — OR FEARED — FOR ITS HEAT AND SPICINESS.

pork fillet	1 kg (2 lb 4 oz)
oil	3 tablespoons
onions	2, finely chopped
garlic	4 cloves, crushed
ginger	1 tablespoon finely chopped
garam masala	1 tablespoon
brown mustard seeds	2 teaspoons
ready-made vindaloo paste	4 tablespoons

Trim the pork fillet of any excess fat and sinew and cut into bite-sized pieces.

Heat the oil in a saucepan, add the meat in small batches and cook over medium heat for 5–7 minutes, or until browned. Remove from the pan.

Add the onion, garlic, ginger, garam masala and mustard seeds to the pan, and cook, stirring, for 5 minutes, or until the onion is soft.

Return all the meat to the pan, add the vindaloo paste and cook, stirring, for 2 minutes. Add 625 ml (21½ fl oz/2½ cups) water and bring to the boil. Reduce the heat and simmer, covered, for 1½ hours, or until the meat is tender.

There are three main varieties of mustard seeds: black, the hottest and most pungent; brown; and white (sometimes called yellow). Mustard has been cultivated for thousands of years and is eaten today in various forms all over the world. In India, in particular, mustard is considered an auspicious ingredient. Whole mustard seeds have little scent — it is only when mixed with a liquid such as water that the seeds release their distinctive aroma and sharp, biting flavour. When fried in oil until they pop, as is common in Indian curry preparations, the seeds take on a nutty taste without the searing heat. Mustard seeds are also available as a paste, powder and oil.

balinese seafood curry . . . . serves 6

THE CHILLI ARRIVED IN BALI FAIRLY RECENTLY — WITH THE PORTUGUESE IN THE SIXTEENTH CENTURY — BUT IT HAS FOUND ITS WAY INTO MOST DISHES. BALINESE CUISINE IS RENOWNED FOR ITS SPICY AND COMPLEX FLAVOURS, ITS LOVE OF FISH AND CAREFUL PREPARATION OF THE SPICE BLEND.

curry paste

coriander seeds	1 tablespoon
shrimp paste	1 teaspoon
tomatoes	2
red chillies	5
garlic	5 cloves, crushed
lemon grass	2 stems, white part only, chopped
ground almonds	1 tablespoon
ground nutmeg	1/4 teaspoon
ground turmeric	1 teaspoon
tamarind purée	60 g (2 1/4 oz/1/4 cup)
lime juice	3 tablespoons
skinless, firm white fish fillets	250 g (9 oz) cut into 3 cm (1 1/4 in) cubes
oil	3 tablespoons
red onions	2, chopped
red chillies	2, seeded, sliced
raw prawns (shrimp)	400 g (14 oz), peeled, deveined, tails intact
squid tubes	250 g (9 oz), cut into 1 cm (1/2 in) rings
fish stock	125 ml (4 fl oz/1/2 cup)
Thai basil	shredded, to serve

Dry-fry the coriander seeds and the shrimp paste wrapped in some foil in a frying pan over medium–high heat for 2–3 minutes, or until fragrant. Allow to cool. Using a mortar with a pestle, or a spice grinder, crush or grind the coriander seeds to a powder.

Score a cross in the base of the tomatoes, place in a heatproof bowl and cover with boiling water. Leave to stand for 30 seconds, then transfer to cold water and peel the skin away from the cross. Cut the tomatoes in half and scoop out the seeds. Discard the seeds and roughly chop the tomato flesh.

Put the crushed coriander seeds, the shrimp paste and tomato with the remaining curry paste ingredients in a food processor, or in a mortar with a pestle, and process or pound to a smooth paste.

Put the lime juice in a bowl and season with salt and freshly ground black pepper. Add the fish, toss to coat well and leave to marinate for 20 minutes.

Heat the oil in a saucepan or wok, add the onion, sliced red chilli and curry paste, and cook, stirring occasionally, over low heat for 10 minutes, or until fragrant. Add the fish and prawns, and stir to coat in the curry paste mixture. Cook for 3 minutes, or until the prawns just turn pink, then add the squid and cook for 1 minute.

Add the stock and bring to the boil, then reduce the heat and simmer for 2 minutes, or until the seafood is cooked and tender. Season to taste with salt and freshly ground black pepper. Top with the shredded basil leaves.

malaysian nonya chicken curry .... serves 4

IN THE FIFTEENTH CENTURY, THE STRAIT OF MALACCA WAS THE FAVOURED ROUTE OF CHINESE TRADERS TO ARABIA AND INDIA. MANY SETTLED IN THE AREA AND MARRIED THE LOCAL WOMEN, WHO BECAME KNOWN AS 'NONYA'. A UNIQUE CUISINE DEVELOPED, WHICH BLENDED CHINESE TECHNIQUES AND MALAYSIAN SPICES.

curry paste

shrimp paste	1/2 teaspoon
red onions	2, chopped
red chillies	4, seeded
garlic	4 cloves, crushed
lemon grass	2 stems, white part only, sliced
galangal	3 cm (1 1/4 in) cube, sliced
makrut (kaffir lime) leaves	8, roughly chopped
ground turmeric	1 teaspoon
oil	2 tablespoons
chicken thigh fillets	750 g (1 lb 10 oz), cut into bite-sized pieces
coconut milk	400 ml (14 fl oz)
tamarind purée	3 1/2 tablespoons
fish sauce	1 tablespoon
makrut (kaffir lime) leaves	3, shredded

Dry-fry the shrimp paste wrapped in some foil in a frying pan over medium–high heat for 2–3 minutes, or until fragrant. Allow to cool.

Put the shrimp paste with the remaining curry paste ingredients in a food processor, or in a mortar with a pestle, and process or pound to a smooth paste.

Heat a wok or large saucepan over high heat, add the oil and swirl to coat the side. Add the curry paste and cook, stirring occasionally, over low heat for 8–10 minutes, or until fragrant. Add the chicken and stir-fry with the paste for 2–3 minutes.

Add the coconut milk, tamarind purée and fish sauce to the wok, and simmer, stirring occasionally, for 15–20 minutes, or until the chicken is tender. Garnish with the shredded makrut leaves and serve.

Put the paste ingredients in a food processor or mortar.

Process or pound the mixture until a smooth paste is formed.

goan fish curry......................................serves 6

GOA IS SITUATED ON INDIA'S SOUTHWEST COAST WHERE SEAFOOD IS A STAPLE INGREDIENT. THE OTHER FAVOURITE INGREDIENT IS COCONUT, AND FEW DISHES ARE WITHOUT IT. DISHES, INCLUDING THIS ONE, ARE TYPICALLY RICH, SIMPLE AND PLEASANTLY SPICY WITH CHILLIES, GINGER, TURMERIC AND TAMARIND.

oil	3 tablespoons
onion	1 large, finely chopped
garlic	4–5 cloves, crushed
ginger	2 teaspoons grated
dried red chillies	4–6
coriander seeds	1 tablespoon
cumin seeds	2 teaspoons
ground turmeric	1 teaspoon
chilli powder	1/4 teaspoon
desiccated coconut	30 g (1 oz/1/3 cup)
coconut milk	270 ml (91/2 fl oz)
tomatoes	2, peeled and chopped
tamarind purée	2 tablespoons
white vinegar	1 tablespoon
curry leaves	6
skinless, firm white fish fillets	1 kg (2 lb 4 oz), cut into 8 cm (31/4 in) pieces

Heat the oil in a large saucepan. Add the onion and cook, stirring, over low heat for 10 minutes, or until softened and lightly golden. Add the garlic and ginger, and cook for a further 2 minutes.

Dry-fry the dried chillies, coriander seeds, cumin seeds, ground turmeric, chilli powder and desiccated coconut in a frying pan over medium–high heat for 2–3 minutes, or until fragrant. Allow to cool. Using a mortar with a pestle, or a spice grinder, crush or grind to a powder.

Add the spice mixture, coconut milk, tomato, tamarind, vinegar and curry leaves to the onion mixture. Stir to mix thoroughly, add 250 ml (9 fl oz/1 cup) water and simmer, stirring frequently, for 10 minutes, or until the tomato has softened and the mixture has thickened slightly.

Add the fish and cook, covered, over low heat for 10 minutes, or until cooked through. Stir gently once or twice during cooking and add a little water if the mixture is too thick.

Dry-fry the spices and desiccated coconut until aromatic.

Use a mortar with a pestle or spice grinder to grind the spices.

Stir the coconut milk into the onion and spice mixture.

three ways with yoghurt

FOR DINERS EATING A FIERY CURRY, YOGHURT IS OFTEN A GREAT SAVIOUR. IT IS USED IN NUMEROUS SIDE DISHES, SPECIFICALLY DESIGNED TO ACCOMPANY SPICY MEALS, AND PERHAPS THE MOST FAMOUS EXAMPLES ARE INDIAN RAITAS. THESE FRESHLY-MADE, SIMPLE YOGHURT PREPARATIONS CAN BE MIXED WITH GRATED VEGETABLES, HERBS, SPICES OR COCONUT — WHATEVER SUITS THE CURRY. EQUALLY CREAMY AND SOOTHING ARE CHURRIS, WHICH ALSO CONTAIN BUTTERMILK, AND CARROT PACHADI, A SLIGHTLY SPICIER BLEND.

churri (yoghurt and buttermilk side dish)

Dry-fry 1 teaspoon cumin seeds in a frying pan over medium–high heat for 2–3 minutes, or until fragrant. Allow to cool. Using a mortar with a pestle, or a spice grinder, crush or grind to a powder. Roughly chop a large handful of mint leaves and coriander leaves. Put the mint and coriander in a food processor with a 2 cm (3/4 in) piece of ginger and 2 green chillies and process to a smooth paste. Add 310 g (11 oz/1 1/4 cups) Greek-style yoghurt, 300 ml (10 1/2 fl oz) buttermilk and a pinch of salt to the mixture and process until all the ingredients are well mixed. Season then mix in 1 thinly sliced onion and the ground cumin, reserving a little cumin to sprinkle on top. Serves 4.

cucumber and tomato raita

Put 450 g (1 lb) grated cucumber and 1 large, finely chopped ripe tomato in a sieve for 20 minutes to drain off any excess liquid. Mix them in a bowl with 310 g (11 oz/1 1/4 cups) Greek-style yoghurt and season to taste with salt. Heat 1/2 tablespoon of oil in a small saucepan over medium heat, add 1 teaspoon of black mustard seeds then cover and shake the pan until the seeds start to pop. Pour the seeds and oil over the yoghurt. Serve sprinkled with chopped coriander leaves. Serves 4.

carrot pachadi (yoghurt and carrot side dish)

Heat 1 tablespoon oil in a small saucepan over medium heat, add 1 teaspoon black mustard seeds and 2–3 dried chillies then cover and shake the pan until the seeds start to pop. Remove from the heat and immediately stir in a pinch of asafoetida and 1 stalk of curry leaves. Whisk 590 g (1 lb 5 oz/2 1/3 cups) Greek-style yoghurt to remove any lumps, then mix in 4 grated carrots. Mix in the mustard seeds, chillies, asafoetida and curry leaves along with the oil, then season with salt, to taste. Garnish with coriander leaves. Serves 4.

churri

beef balls with pickled garlic

THIS DISH INVOLVES LITTLE PREPARATION, MAKING IT A WELCOME CHOICE WHEN YOU FEEL LIKE A CURRY BUT CAN'T BE BOTHERED WITH THE GRINDING AND ROASTING. PICKLED GARLIC HAS A SWEET–SOUR FLAVOUR AND IS USED IN CURRIES AS A MEANS OF BALANCING OTHER FLAVOURS — BE THEY HOT, CREAMY OR SWEET.

meatballs

minced (ground) beef	450 g (1 lb)
garlic	3 cloves, crushed
white pepper	1 teaspoon
coriander (cilantro)	1 small handful leaves, chopped
Thai basil	1 small handful, chopped
spring onion (scallion)	1, finely chopped
fish sauce	3 teaspoons
egg	1
oil	3 tablespoons
green curry paste	3 tablespoons, ready-made or see recipe on page 130
ginger	3 tablespoons finely chopped
ground turmeric	1 1/2 teaspoons
fish sauce	3 tablespoons
makrut (kaffir lime) leaves	3
tamarind purée	2 1/2 tablespoons
pickled garlic	3 tablespoons chopped
palm sugar (jaggery)	1 1/2 tablespoons shaved

To make the meatballs, combine all the ingredients together well. Then, taking a tablespoon at a time, roll the mixture into small balls. You should have about 24 balls.

Heat the oil in a heavy-based saucepan over medium heat and add the curry paste, ginger and turmeric and cook, stirring frequently for about 5 minutes, or until fragrant.

Add the fish sauce, makrut leaves and tamarind. Bring to the boil then cover, reduce to a simmer and cook for 5 minutes. Add the meatballs, pickled garlic and palm sugar and simmer for 15 minutes, or until meatballs are cooked through.

Roll tablespoons of the mince mixture into 24 balls.

Add the meatballs to the sauce and simmer until cooked through.

malaysian hot and sour pineapple curry . . . . serves 6

PINEAPPLE ADDS A TOUCH OF TART SWEETNESS TO CURRIES AND IS POPULAR IN VEGETARIAN MEALS. HERE, IT IS MIXED WITH HOT CHILLIES, CREAMY COCONUT AND THE MELLOW WARMTH OF CLOVES AND CINNAMON TO PRODUCE A REFRESHING DISH THAT IS A LITTLE BIT SWEET AND A LITTLE BIT SPICY.

pineapple	1 semi-ripe, cored, cut into chunks
ground turmeric	1/2 teaspoon
star anise	1
cinnamon stick	1, broken into small pieces
cloves	7
cardamom pods	7, bruised
oil	1 tablespoon
onion	1, finely chopped
ginger	1 teaspoon grated
garlic	1 clove, crushed
red chillies	5, chopped
sugar	1 tablespoon
coconut cream	3 tablespoons

Put the pineapple in a saucepan, cover with water and add the turmeric. Put the star anise, cinnamon, cloves and cardamom pods on a square of muslin, and tie securely with string. Add to the pan and cook over medium heat for 10 minutes. Squeeze the bag to extract any flavour, then discard. Reserve the cooking liquid.

Heat the oil in a frying pan, add the onion, ginger, garlic and chilli, and cook, stirring, for 1–2 minutes, or until fragrant. Add the pineapple and the cooking liquid, sugar and salt to taste. Cook for 2 minutes, then stir in the coconut cream. Cook, stirring, over low heat for 3–5 minutes, or until the sauce thickens. Serve this curry hot or cold.

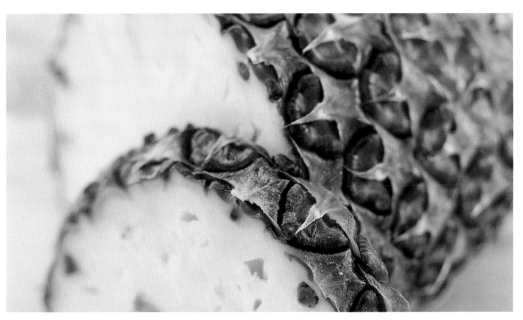

A native of tropical South America, the pineapple is actually several individual fruit joined together: each of these fruit are the result of numerous unfertilized flowers fused together. To most of us, however, it is a deliciously juicy and sweet fruit, the very emblem of warm weather. Like most fruit, pineapple is best eaten fresh, but it is also used in dishes such as curries, ice creams, sorbets and cakes. Pineapples do not carry on ripening after being picked, so it pays to choose well. Select ones that are heavy for their size and sweetly aromatic.

tamarind fish curry
serves 4

TAMARIND IS WIDELY USED IN INDIAN AND SOUTHEAST ASIAN COOKING FOR ITS SWEET–SOUR FLAVOUR AND SOURING PROPERTIES. HERE, THE TAMARIND IS BALANCED BY FULL-BODIED PEPPERCORNS, CUMIN AND CORIANDER; MADE AROMATIC WITH PUNGENT SAFFRON AND SWEET CARDAMOM; AND CREAMY WITH THICK YOGHURT.

skinless, firm white fish fillets	600 g (1 lb 5 oz)
turmeric	1 teaspoon
powdered saffron	pinch
garlic	3 cloves, crushed
lemon juice	2 teaspoons
cumin seeds	1 teaspoon
coriander seeds	2 tablespoons
white peppercorns	1 teaspoon
cardamom pods	4, bruised
ginger	2 1/2 tablespoons finely chopped
red chillies	2, finely sliced
oil	2 tablespoons
onion	1, chopped
red capsicum (pepper)	1, cut into 2 cm (3/4 in) squares
green capsicum (pepper)	1, cut into 2 cm (3/4 in) squares
Roma (plum) tomatoes	4, diced
tamarind purée	2 tablespoons
plain yoghurt	185 g (6 1/2 oz/3/4 cup)
coriander (cilantro)	2 tablespoons chopped leaves

Rinse the fish fillets and pat dry. Prick the fillets with a fork. Combine the turmeric, saffron, garlic, lemon juice and 1 teaspoon of salt then rub over the fish fillets. Refrigerate for 2–3 hours.

Dry-fry the cumin seeds, coriander seeds, peppercorns and cardamom in a frying pan over medium–high heat for 2–3 minutes, or until fragrant. Allow to cool. Using a mortar with a pestle, or a spice grinder, crush or grind to a powder and combine with the ginger and chillies.

Heat the oil in a heavy-based saucepan over medium heat and add the chopped onion, red and green capsicum, and ground spice mix. Cook gently for 10 minutes, or until aromatic and the onion is transparent. Increase heat to high, add the diced tomatoes, 250 ml (9 fl oz/1 cup) of water and the tamarind purée. Bring to the boil then reduce to a simmer and cook for 20 minutes.

Rinse the paste off the fish and chop into 3 cm (1 1/4 in) pieces. Add to the pan and continue to simmer for 10 minutes. Stir in the yoghurt and chopped coriander and serve.

Rub the saffron mixture into the fish fillets and leave for 2–3 hours.

Dry-fry the spices until aromatic then grind to a fine powder.

Add the onion, capsicum and spice mix to the saucepan.

pork and bitter melon curry................................serves 4

THIS IS AN IMPRESSIVE LOOKING CURRY, WITH ITS STUFFED BITTER MELON COMMANDING ATTENTION. IN THIS DISH, THIS DISTINCTIVE VEGETABLE IS BALANCED BY OTHER STRONG FLAVOURS, INCLUDING PORK, GARLIC AND CHILLIES. DESPITE ITS NAME, BITTER MELON IS ACTUALLY QUITE DELICIOUS.

bitter melon	6, about 700 g (1 lb 9 oz) total
sugar	2 tablespoons

pork filling

minced (ground) pork	250 g (9 oz)
ginger	1 teaspoon chopped
white peppercorns	1/2 teaspoon, crushed
garlic	1 clove, crushed
spring onion (scallion)	1, finely chopped
paprika	1 teaspoon
water chestnuts	2 tablespoons finely chopped
makrut (kaffir lime) leaves	2, thinly sliced
crushed peanuts	1 1/2 tablespoons
coriander (cilantro)	1 small handful leaves, chopped
palm sugar (jaggery)	1 tablespoon shaved
fish sauce	1 tablespoon

oil	3 tablespoons
red curry paste	2 tablespoons, ready-made or see recipe on page 18
palm sugar (jaggery)	1 tablespoon shaved
fish sauce	2 tablespoons
coconut cream	250 ml (9 fl oz/1 cup)
makrut (kaffir lime) leaves	4

Discard the ends of the bitter melon then cut into 2.5 cm (1 in) slices. Hollow out the fibrous centre membrane and seeds with a small knife, leaving the outside rings intact. Bring 750 ml (26 fl oz/3 cups) water to the boil with the sugar and 3 teaspoons salt. Blanch the melon for 2 minutes and drain.

Combine all ingredients for the pork filling. Pack this into the melon pieces. Heat 2 tablespoons of the oil in a heavy-based saucepan over low heat and add the melon, cooking for 3 minutes on each side, or until pork is golden and sealed. Set the pieces aside.

Add the remaining oil to the pan with the red curry paste. Stir for 3 minutes, or until aromatic. Add the palm sugar and fish sauce and stir until dissolved. Add the coconut cream, 250 ml (9 fl oz/ 1 cup) water and makrut leaves. Simmer for 5 minutes, then carefully add the bitter melon. Continue simmering, turning pork halfway through, for 20 minutes, or until pork is cooked and the melon is tender.

Note: Telegraph (long) cucumbers can be used instead of bitter melon. Follow the same method above.

Cut the bitter melon into slices and hollow out the centre.

Pack the pork filling into the bitter melon slices.

hot and sour eggplant curry

EGGPLANT (AUBERGINE) GOES PARTICULARLY WELL WITH CORIANDER, CUMIN AND COCONUT — RICH, WARM FLAVOURS — BUT IS SURPRISINGLY AMENABLE TO A WIDE RANGE OF INGREDIENTS, SUCH AS THE CURRY-SCENTED FENUGREEK AND ANISE-FLAVOURED FENNEL USED IN THIS DISH.

eggplant (aubergine)	1 large (about 500 g/1 lb 2 oz)
tomatoes	2 small
oil	2 tablespoons
fenugreek seeds	3 teaspoons
fennel seeds	3 teaspoons
garlic	4 cloves, crushed
onion	1 large, finely diced
curry leaves	4
ground coriander	1 1/2 tablespoons
turmeric	2 teaspoons
tomato juice	125 ml (4 fl oz/1/2 cup)
tamarind purée	2 tablespoons
red chillies	2, finely sliced
coconut cream	125 ml (4 fl oz/1/2 cup)
coriander (cilantro)	1 handful leaves, chopped

Cut the eggplant into 2 cm (3/4 in) cubes. Sprinkle with 1/2 teaspoon salt and set aside for 1 hour. Drain and rinse.

Chop the tomatoes into rough dice. Heat the oil in a heavy-based saucepan over medium heat. Add the fenugreek and fennel seeds. When they start to crackle, add the garlic, onion and curry leaves and cook for 3–5 minutes or until onion is transparent. Add the eggplant and stir for 6 minutes, or until it begins to soften. Add the ground spices, tomatoes, tomato juice, tamarind and sliced fresh chillies.

Bring to the boil, then reduce to a simmer, cover and continue to cook for about 35 minutes, or until eggplant is very soft. Stir in the coconut cream and coriander and season to taste.

Chop the tomatoes into a rough dice, keeping the skin and seeds.

Cook the onion for 3–5 minutes, or until it becomes transparent.

When the eggplant is very soft, stir in the coconut cream.

the perfect rice

Anywhere there is curry, rice will be close to hand. Although there are three basic rice types available, only long-grain is considered the natural accompaniment to curries. Compared with short- and medium-grain rices, long-grain is generally thinner, longer, less starchy and when cooked yields a light fluffy, loose-grained texture. There are several varieties of long-grain rice and although, at a pinch, any will do the trick, for authenticity try serving the dry, separate grained, nutty-tasting basmati rice with Indian curries and aromatic, slightly clingy, floral scented jasmine rice alongside Thai curries. The flavours of both these rice varieties complement the spices in the curries from the corresponding cuisines.

Absorption method

Put the rice in a saucepan and shake so that it evenly coats the bottom of the pan. Stick the very tip of your finger into the rice then add enough cold water to come up to the first finger joint. Bring to the boil over high heat then cover with a clear, tight-fitting lid. Reduce heat to low and cook until the water has mostly evaporated and small steam holes appear on the surface of the rice. Remove the lid, fluff with a fork and serve.

Rapid boil method

Bring a large saucepan of water to the boil over high heat. Sprinkle over the rice and cook according to the instructions on the packet or until the grains are tender. Drain the rice in a colander. If using jasmine rice, which is slightly glutinous, rinse with a little tepid water before serving.

balti-style lamb .... serves 4

BALTISTAN MAY LIE HIGH IN THE MOUNTAINS OF NORTH PAKISTAN, BUT BIRMINGHAM, ENGLAND, HAS BECOME THE INTERNATIONAL LAUNCH PAD OF BALTI CUISINE. DISTINCTIVE FOR ITS USE OF THE TWO-HANDLED *KARAHI* POT, IT ALSO FEATURES ITS OWN MASALA PASTE, WHICH IS HERBY AND FRAGRANT WITH GREEN CARDAMOM.

lamb leg steaks	1 kg (2 lb 4 oz), cut into 3 cm (1¼ in) cubes
ready-made balti masala paste	5 tablespoons
ghee or oil	2 tablespoons
garlic	3 cloves, crushed
garam masala	1 tablespoon
onion	1 large, finely chopped
coriander (cilantro)	2 tablespoons chopped leaves, plus extra for garnish

Preheat the oven to 190°C (375°F/Gas 5). Put the meat, 1 tablespoon of the balti masala paste and 375 ml (13 fl oz/ 1½ cups) boiling water in a large casserole dish or karahi, and combine. Cook, covered, in the oven for 30–40 minutes, or until almost cooked through. Drain, reserving the stock.

Heat the ghee or oil in a wok, add the garlic and garam masala, and stir-fry over medium heat for 1 minute. Add the onion and cook for 5–7 minutes, or until the onion is soft and golden brown. Increase the heat, add the remaining balti masala paste and the lamb. Cook for 5 minutes to brown the meat. Slowly add the reserved stock and simmer over low heat, stirring occasionally, for 15 minutes.

Add the chopped coriander leaves and 185 ml (6 fl oz/¾ cup) water and simmer for 15 minutes, or until the meat is tender and the sauce has thickened slightly. Season with salt and freshly ground black pepper and garnish with extra coriander leaves.

Ghee is most often associated with Indian cooking, but its usefulness as a cooking medium means it is now used throughout Southeast Asia. It is a clarified butter — that is, butter that has been melted and boiled to remove milk solids and water. The resulting ghee has a high burning point, little moisture and a high fat content, so a little goes a long way. Most importantly, ghee has a strong nutty flavour and rich, toasted aroma, which is used to advantage in meat and vegetable curries, lentil dals and rice dishes. Buy from Asian and Indian food stores and store in a cool, dark place.

duck and coconut curry............................serves 6

THE USE OF SOUR VINEGAR IN A CURRY MAY SEEM AN UNUSUAL ADDITION, BUT IT CAN PROVIDE AN EXCELLENT FOIL FOR RICH COCONUT MILK AND FATTY MEAT SUCH AS DUCK. IN INDIA, IT IS OFTEN FOUND IN REGIONAL COOKING THAT HAS BEEN INFLUENCED BY OTHER CULTURES, SUCH AS THE FOOD OF GOA AND THE PARSEES.

curry paste

coriander seeds	1 1/2 teaspoons
cardamom seeds	1 teaspoon
fenugreek seeds	1 teaspoon
brown mustard seeds	1 teaspoon
black peppercorns	10
red onion	1, chopped
garlic	2 cloves, crushed
red chillies	4, seeded, chopped
coriander (cilantro)	2 roots, chopped
ginger	2 teaspoons grated
garam masala	2 teaspoons
ground turmeric	1/4 teaspoon
tamarind purée	2 teaspoons
duck breast fillets	6
red onion	1, sliced
white vinegar	125 ml (4 fl oz/1/2 cup)
coconut milk	500 ml (17 fl oz/2 cups)
coriander (cilantro)	1 small handful leaves

Dry-fry the coriander, cardamom, fenugreek and mustard seeds in a frying pan over medium–high heat for 2–3 minutes, or until fragrant. Allow to cool. Using a mortar with a pestle, or a spice grinder, crush or grind the spices with the black peppercorns to a powder.

Put the ground spices with the remaining curry paste ingredients in a food processor, or in a mortar with a pestle, and process or pound to a smooth paste.

Trim any excess fat from the duck fillets, then place, skin side down, in a large saucepan and cook over medium heat for 10 minutes, or until the skin is brown and any remaining fat has melted. Turn the fillets over and cook for 5 minutes, or until tender. Remove and drain on paper towel.

Reserve 1 tablespoon duck fat, discard the remaining fat. Add the onion and cook for 5 minutes, then add the curry paste and stir over low heat for 10 minutes, or until fragrant.

Return the duck to the pan and stir to coat with the paste. Stir in the vinegar, coconut milk, 1 teaspoon salt and 125 ml (4 fl oz/ 1/2 cup) water. Simmer, covered, for 45 minutes, or until the fillets are tender. Stir in the coriander leaves just prior to serving.

Process the onion, garlic, spices and tamarind until smooth.

Trim the excess fat from the duck fillets before adding to the pan.

sour lamb and bamboo curry ....serves 4

BAMBOO SHOOTS ARE USED MAINLY IN SOUTHEAST ASIAN COOKING. WHEN FRESH, THEY HAVE A LOVELY CRISP, NUTTY BITTERNESS TO THEM. THEY ARE AVAILABLE IN ASIAN FOOD STORES, BUT THE TINNED VARIETY MAKES AN ACCEPTABLE SUBSTITUTE. ALONG WITH THE GREEN BEANS AND LAMB, THEY PROVIDE TEXTURE TO THIS CURRY.

curry paste

white peppercorns	1 teaspoon
shrimp paste	1 teaspoon
dried shrimp	30 g (1 oz)
spring onions (scallions)	6, sliced
jalapeño chillies (in brine)	60 g (2¼ oz) sliced
lemon grass	2 stems, white part only, thinly sliced
garlic	6 cloves, crushed
coriander (cilantro)	4 roots, chopped
ground galangal	2 teaspoons
chilli powder	1 teaspoon
fish sauce	80 ml (2½ fl oz/⅓ cup)
lime juice	80 ml (2½ fl oz/⅓ cup)
ground turmeric	1 teaspoon
boneless lamb leg	500 g (1 lb 2 oz), trimmed of excess fat
oil	1 tablespoon
palm sugar (jaggery)	1 tablespoon shaved
coconut cream	250 ml (9 fl oz/1 cup)
tamarind purée	60 g (2¼ oz/¼ cup)
fish sauce	1½ tablespoons
bamboo shoot pieces	400 g (14 oz) tinned, cut into thick wedges
green beans	200 g (7 oz), cut into 4 cm (1½ in) lengths

Dry-fry the peppercorns and the shrimp paste wrapped in some foil in a frying pan over medium–high heat for 2–3 minutes, or until fragrant. Allow to cool. Using a mortar with a pestle, or a spice grinder, crush or grind to a powder. Process the dried shrimp in a food processor until it becomes very finely shredded — forming a 'floss'.

Put the crushed peppercorns, shrimp paste and dried shrimp with the remaining curry paste ingredients in a food processor, or in a mortar with a pestle, and process or pound to a smooth paste.

Slice the lamb into strips 5 x 2 cm (2 x ¾ in) and 3 mm (⅛ in) thick. Heat the oil in a heavy-based casserole dish over medium heat and add 2–3 tablespoons of paste. Stir constantly, adding the palm sugar. When the palm sugar has dissolved add the lamb, stirring for about 7 minutes, or until lightly golden.

Add the coconut cream, 250 ml (9 fl oz/1 cup) water, tamarind, fish sauce and bamboo. Bring to the boil then reduce heat and simmer for about 20 minutes, or until tender. Add the beans and simmer for a further 3 minutes. Season to taste and serve.

thai hot and sour
prawn and pumpkin curry . . . . serves 4

FLAVOURED WITH RED CURRY PASTE, PERFUMED BY MAKRUT (KAFFIR LIME) LEAVES, AND SEASONED WITH TAMARIND, FISH SAUCE, LIME JUICE AND CHILLIES, THIS DELICIOUS CURRY IS A REAL MEAL-IN-A-BOWL. THE FLAVOURS ARE WELL-BALANCED, WITH A BIT OF BITE AND A LOVELY TANGY TASTE, BUT DO NOT OVERPOWER THE PRAWNS (SHRIMP).

jap pumpkin (kent squash)	250 g (9 oz)
Lebanese (short) cucumber	1
coconut cream	400 ml (14 fl oz/1²/₃ cups) (do not shake the tin)
red curry paste	1¹/₂ tablespoons, ready-made or see recipe on page 18
fish sauce	3 tablespoons
palm sugar (jaggery)	2 tablespoons shaved
straw mushrooms	400 g (14 oz) tinned, drained
raw prawns (shrimp)	500 g (1 lb 2 oz), peeled, deveined, tails intact
tamarind purée	2 tablespoons
red chillies	2, chopped
lime juice	1 tablespoon
makrut (kaffir lime) leaves	4
coriander (cilantro)	4 roots, chopped
bean sprouts	1 small handful, to serve
coriander (cilantro)	1 small handful leaves, to serve

Peel the pumpkin and chop into 2 cm (³/₄ in) cubes. Peel and cut the cucumber in half lengthways, then scrape out the seeds with a teaspoon and thinly slice.

Put the thick coconut cream from the top of the tin in a saucepan, bring to a rapid simmer over medium heat, stirring occasionally, and cook for 5–10 minutes, or until the mixture 'splits' (the oil starts to separate). Add the paste and stir for 2–3 minutes, or until fragrant. Add the fish sauce and palm sugar and stir until dissolved.

Add the remaining coconut cream, pumpkin, and 3 tablespoons of water, cover and bring to boil. Reduce to a simmer and cook for 10 minutes, or until pumpkin is just starting to become tender. Add the straw mushrooms, prawns, cucumber, tamarind, chilli, lime juice, makrut leaves and coriander roots. Cover, increase the heat and bring to the boil again before reducing to a simmer and cooking for 3–5 minutes, or until the prawns are just cooked through. Garnish with bean sprouts and coriander leaves.

It's hard to believe chillies aren't indigenous to Asia, such is their importance in cuisines stretching from India to Indonesia. However, since their introduction to the region in the sixteenth century, they have become inextricably linked with the local diets. There are thousands of varieties of chilli plants, with pods in an assortment of shapes, sizes and colours, and varying in their degree of hotness from gentle to positively painful. But chillies are not merely hot; each has its own flavour, and dried and fresh chillies also taste very different. Some popular varieties used in curries include cayenne, kashmiri and bird's eye chillies.

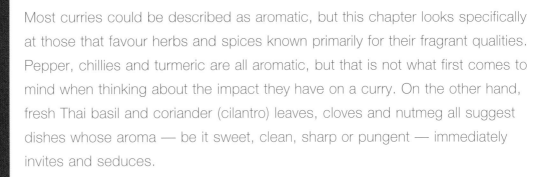

Most curries could be described as aromatic, but this chapter looks specifically at those that favour herbs and spices known primarily for their fragrant qualities. Pepper, chillies and turmeric are all aromatic, but that is not what first comes to mind when thinking about the impact they have on a curry. On the other hand, fresh Thai basil and coriander (cilantro) leaves, cloves and nutmeg all suggest dishes whose aroma — be it sweet, clean, sharp or pungent — immediately invites and seduces.

Thai cooking in particular makes good use of fresh herbs to engage the sense of smell. If Indian cooking excels at combining dried spices, Thai cooking delights in creating curries with layers of flavour and aroma from a wide range of fresh herbs, spices and seasonings. These include local ingredients such as the aniseed-like Thai basil, floral makrut (kaffir lime) leaves and tangy galangal, as well as more familiar ones such as coriander, ginger, lemon grass, garlic, spring onions (scallions) and onions. It is sometimes easy to overlook the importance of these reliable stalwarts, but few curries could do without the body and flavour they provide, as well as their sharp, clean and sweet aromas.

A Thai green curry is the classic example of this art, blending most of the above with chicken, vegetables or fish in a coconut-based sauce with green chillies for heat. The finished dish — tart, salty and hot — is generously garnished with fresh-tasting, fragrant makrut and Thai basil leaves. Thai curries are renowned for the care taken with the preparation and cooking of ingredients, and the frying of the curry paste is a careful exercise in letting your nose tell you when to add the next ingredient. Learning to recognize the different aromas of herbs and spices is not essential for the occasional curry cook — you'll still produce delicious results — but is certainly something dedicated lovers of curries aspire to.

Apart from a number of Thai curries, this chapter also features various Indian curries, including spicy and fragrant fish koftas, a lamb and spinach curry, whose heady blend of cumin, coriander seeds, black peppercorns, Indian bay (cassia) leaves, garam masala, turmeric and paprika is classically Indian and extremely inviting. Finally, there is also a dum aloo, which is based on a traditional method of steaming ingredients in their own juices and flavourings. Fragrant with cardamom, cloves, cinnamon, ginger, cumin and chillies, the aromas will be tempting you long before the dish is on the table.

spiced chicken with almonds . . . . serves 6

THIS IS A WONDERFULLY SIMPLE AND AROMATIC DISH, WITH LITTLE OF THE SHARPNESS OR SPICINESS FOUND IN MANY CURRIES. ALMONDS WERE FIRST INTRODUCED TO INDIA BY THE MOGHUL EMPERORS AND REMAIN ASSOCIATED WITH SUMPTUOUS DINING. IN THIS DISH, THEY ARE USED BOTH IN THE SAUCE AND AS A GARNISH.

oil	3 tablespoons
slivered almonds	30 g (1 oz/¼ cup)
red onions	2, finely chopped
garlic	4–6 cloves, crushed
ginger	1 tablespoon grated
cardamom pods	4, bruised
cloves	4
ground cumin	1 teaspoon
ground coriander	1 teaspoon
ground turmeric	1 teaspoon
chilli powder	½ teaspoon
chicken thigh fillets	1 kg (2 lb 4 oz), trimmed
tomatoes	2 large, peeled, chopped
cinnamon stick	1
ground almonds	100 g (3½ oz/1 cup)

Heat 1 tablespoon oil in a large saucepan. Add the almonds and cook over low heat for 15 seconds, or until lightly golden brown. Remove and drain on crumpled paper towel.

Heat the remaining oil, add the onion, and cook, stirring, for 8 minutes, or until golden brown. Add the garlic and ginger and cook, stirring, for 2 minutes, then stir in the spices. Reduce the heat to low and cook for 2 minutes, or until aromatic.

Add the chicken and cook, stirring constantly, for 5 minutes, or until well coated with the spices and starting to colour.

Stir in the tomato, cinnamon stick, ground almonds and 250 ml (9 fl oz/1 cup) hot water. Simmer, covered, over low heat for 1 hour, or until the chicken is cooked through and tender. Stir often and add a little more water, if needed.

Leave the pan to stand, covered, for 30 minutes for the flavours to develop, then remove the cinnamon stick. Scatter the slivered almonds over the top and serve.

Cook the almonds until lightly golden then set aside and drain.

Toss the chicken pieces in the spices, coating well.

Add the tomato, cinnamon and ground almonds and simmer.

creamy prawn curry..serves 4

CREAMY, YES, BUT ALSO FRAGRANT WITH CLOVES, CARDAMOM, CINNAMON AND INDIAN BAY LEAVES. MAKE SURE YOU USE INDIAN BAY LEAVES AND NOT THE EUROPEAN VARIETY. THEY SHOULD MORE ACCURATELY BE CALLED CASSIA LEAVES, AS THEY ARE FROM THAT TREE. THEY ARE SPICY AND REFRESHING, WITH A SWEET, WOODY AROMA.

tiger prawns (shrimp)	500 g (1 lb 2 oz), peeled, deveined, with tails intact
lemon juice	1$\frac{1}{2}$ tablespoons
oil	3 tablespoons
onion	$\frac{1}{2}$, finely chopped
ground turmeric	$\frac{1}{2}$ teaspoon
cinnamon stick	1
cloves	4
cardamom pods	7, bruised
Indian bay (cassia) leaves	5
ginger	2 cm ($\frac{3}{4}$ in) piece, grated
garlic	3 cloves, crushed
chilli powder	1 teaspoon
coconut milk	170 ml (5$\frac{1}{2}$ fl oz/$\frac{2}{3}$ cup)

Put the prawns in a bowl, add the lemon juice, then toss together and leave them for 5 minutes. Rinse the prawns under running cold water and pat dry with paper towel.

Heat the oil in a heavy-based frying pan and fry the onion until lightly browned. Add the turmeric, cinnamon, cloves, cardamom, bay leaves, ginger and garlic, and fry for 1 minute. Add the chilli powder, coconut milk, and salt to taste, and slowly bring to the boil. Reduce the heat and simmer for 2 minutes.

Add the prawns, return to the boil, then reduce the heat and simmer for 5 minutes, or until the prawns are cooked through and the sauce is thick.

Add the spices to the browned onion and cook until fragrant.

Simmer the prawns gently until just curled and cooked through.

pork and cardamom curry . . . . serves 6

TENDER, SWEET PORK FILLET IS PERFECT FOR THIS DISH: IT IS FAT-FREE, SO NEEDS AN INITIAL BRIEF COOKING TO SEAL IN THE JUICES, BUT THEN WILL COOK FAIRLY QUICKLY IN THE CURRY. THE SPICES — PEPPERCORNS, GINGER, CARDAMOM, CUMIN, GARAM MASALA — COMBINE TO GIVE THIS DISH A LOVELY WARM, EXOTIC FLAVOUR.

curry paste

cardamom pods	10
ginger	6 cm (2½ in) piece, chopped
garlic	3 cloves, crushed
black peppercorns	2 teaspoons
cinnamon stick	1
onion	1, finely sliced
ground cumin	1 teaspoon
ground coriander	1 teaspoon
garam masala	1 teaspoon
oil	3 tablespoons
pork fillet	1 kg (2 lb 4 oz), thinly sliced
tomatoes	2, finely diced
chicken stock	125 ml (4 fl oz/½ cup)
coconut milk	125 ml (4 fl oz/½ cup)

Lightly crush the cardamom pods with the flat side of a heavy knife. Remove the seeds, discarding the pods. Put the seeds and the remaining curry paste ingredients in a food processor, or in a mortar with a pestle, and process or pound to a smooth paste.

Put 2½ tablespoons of oil in a large heavy-based frying pan, and fry the pork in batches until browned, then set aside. Add the remaining oil to the pan, then add the curry paste and cook over medium–high heat for 3–4 minutes, or until aromatic. Add the tomato, chicken stock and coconut milk, and simmer covered over low–medium heat for 15 minutes. While cooking, skim any oil that comes to the surface and discard.

Add the pork to the sauce, and simmer uncovered for 5 minutes, or until cooked. Season well to taste and serve.

Warm and pungent, with lemony undertones, cardamom has been chewed as a breath freshener from the time of the ancient Egyptians to today. Many varieties of cardamom are grown, but the smooth green pods from their native southern India and Sri Lanka are considered the best. Also of note are the large, wrinkled black (brown) pods, which have a coarser flavour. Green cardamom is difficult to harvest, making it expensive and highly valued. It is used in both sweet and savoury Indian and Asian dishes, and both black and green cardamom are essential components of garam masala. Green cardamom is sometimes bleached to form white cardamom.

dum aloo . . . . serves 6

IN INDIA, 'DUM' MEANS TO COOK BY STEAMING — IT TRANSLATES AS 'TO BREATHE IN'. THE TRADITIONAL METHOD WAS TO FILL A POT WITH INGREDIENTS, SEAL THE LID WITH DOUGH AND THEN SET THE POT OVER COALS. THE FOOD WOULD SLOWLY AND DELICATELY COOK IN ITS OWN STEAM AND JUICES.

curry paste

cardamom pods	4
ginger	1 teaspoon grated
garlic	2 cloves, crushed
red chillies	3
cumin seeds	1 teaspoon
cashew nuts	40 g (1 1/2 oz/1/4 cup)
white poppy seeds	1 tablespoon
cinnamon stick	1
cloves	6
all-purpose potatoes	1 kg (2 lb 4 oz), cubed
onions	2, roughly chopped
oil	2 tablespoons
ground turmeric	1/2 teaspoon
besan (chickpea flour)	1 teaspoon
plain yoghurt	250 g (9 oz/1 cup)
coriander (cilantro)	leaves, to garnish

Lightly crush the cardamom pods with the flat side of a heavy knife. Remove the seeds, discarding the pods. Put the seeds and the remaining curry paste ingredients in a food processor, or in a mortar with a pestle, and process or pound to a smooth paste.

Bring a large saucepan of lightly salted water to the boil. Add the potato and cook for 5–6 minutes, or until just tender, then drain.

Put the onions in a food processor and process in short bursts until it is finely chopped but not puréed. Heat the oil in a large saucepan, add the onion and cook over low heat for 5 minutes. Add the curry paste and cook, stirring, for a further 5 minutes, or until fragrant. Stir in the potato, turmeric, salt to taste and 250 ml (9 fl oz/1 cup) water.

Reduce the heat and simmer, tightly covered, for 10 minutes, or until the potato is cooked but not breaking up and the sauce has thickened slightly.

Combine the besan with the yoghurt, add to the potato mixture and cook, stirring, over low heat for 5 minutes, or until thickened again. Garnish with the coriander leaves and serve.

Lightly crush the cardamom pods to release the seeds.

Pulse the onions in a food processor until finely chopped.

Stir in the yoghurt mixture and cook until thickened.

indonesian chicken in coconut milk . . . . serves 6

THIS HEADY DISH PERFECTLY CONJURES UP INDONESIA'S TROPICAL CLIMATE AND PRODUCE. CURRIES ARE TYPICALLY RICH, RELYING ON INGREDIENTS SUCH AS PEPPER, GALANGAL, CORIANDER AND SHRIMP PASTE FOR HOT, TANGY AND SALTY ELEMENTS. NUTMEG, THOUGH NATIVE TO THE AREA, IS A SURPRISINGLY RARE CURRY ADDITION.

curry paste

coriander seeds	2 teaspoons
cumin seeds	1/2 teaspoon
white peppercorns	2 teaspoons
shrimp paste	1/2 teaspoon
lemon grass	2 stems, white part only, sliced
red onions	2, chopped
garlic	3 cloves, crushed
ginger	1 tablespoon grated
galangal	2 1/2 tablespoons grated
ground nutmeg	1/4 teaspoon
ground cloves	1/4 teaspoon
coconut cream	560 ml (19 1/4 fl oz/2 1/4 cups)
chicken	1.5 kg (3 lb 5 oz), cut into 8–10 pieces
coconut milk	800 ml (28 fl oz/3 1/4 cups)
tamarind purée	2 tablespoons
white vinegar	1 tablespoon
cinnamon stick	1

Dry-fry the coriander seeds, cumin seeds, white peppercorns and the shrimp paste wrapped in some foil in a frying pan over medium–high heat for 2–3 minutes, or until fragrant. Allow to cool. Using a mortar with a pestle, or a spice grinder, crush or grind the coriander, cumin and peppercorns to a powder. Process the shrimp in a food processor until it becomes very finely shredded — forming a 'floss'.

Put the crushed spices and the shrimp with the remaining curry paste ingredients in a food processor, or in a mortar with a pestle, and process or pound to a smooth paste.

Heat a large saucepan or wok over medium heat, add the coconut cream and curry paste, and cook, stirring, for 20 minutes, or until thick and oily.

Add the chicken and the remaining ingredients and simmer gently for 50 minutes, or until the chicken is tender. Season to taste and serve immediately.

Not to be confused with the juice found inside a coconut (coconut water), coconut milk/cream is the liquid obtained by pressing the grated flesh of a coconut. Traditionally, water is used in the process, with each subsequent pressing (up to three) producing a thinner milk. In countries where coconut milk is used on a daily basis, the various pressings have specific uses in cooking — a much more sophisticated use than we can get from the humble tinned variety. However, it is still worth shopping around for the best — coconut milk should have a clean, white colour, with the heavier cream on top, and a pleasant flavour free of aftertaste.

thai green chicken curry . . . . serves 4–6

THIS DISH IS A CLASSIC OF THAI COOKING. IT IS HOT AND FRAGRANT FROM THE CURRY PASTE AND PERFUMED WITH MAKRUT (KAFFIR LIME) LEAVES AND THAI BASIL. GREEN PASTES CAN VARY, BUT THEY SHOULD BE PUNGENT RATHER THAN PIERCINGLY HOT, AND BUILT AROUND CHILLIES, GALANGAL, CORIANDER (CILANTRO) AND LEMON GRASS.

green curry paste

white peppercorns	1 teaspoon
coriander seeds	2 tablespoons
cumin seeds	1 teaspoon
shrimp paste	2 teaspoons
sea salt	1 teaspoon
lemon grass	4 stems, white part only, finely sliced
galangal	2 teaspoons chopped
makrut (kaffir lime) leaf	1, finely shredded
coriander (cilantro)	1 tablespoon chopped root
red Asian shallots	5, chopped
garlic	10 cloves, crushed
long green chillies	16, seeded, chopped
coconut cream	500 ml (17 fl oz/2 cups) (do not shake the tins)
palm sugar (jaggery)	2 tablespoons shaved
fish sauce	2 tablespoons
makrut (kaffir lime) leaves	4, finely shredded
chicken thigh or breast fillets	1 kg (2 lb 4 oz), cut into thick strips
bamboo shoots	200 g (7 oz), cut into thick strips
snake (yard-long) beans	100 g (3½ oz), cut into 5 cm (2 in) lengths
Thai basil	1 handful

Dry-fry the peppercorns, coriander seeds, cumin seeds and shrimp paste wrapped in foil in a frying pan over medium–high heat for 2–3 minutes, or until fragrant. Allow to cool. Using a mortar with a pestle, or a spice grinder, crush or grind the peppercorns, coriander and cumin to a powder.

Put the shrimp paste and ground spices with the remaining curry paste ingredients in a food processor, or in a mortar with a pestle, and process or pound to a smooth paste.

Put the thick coconut cream from the top of the tins in a saucepan, bring to a rapid simmer over medium heat, stirring occasionally, and cook for 5–10 minutes, or until the mixture 'splits' (the oil starts to separate).

Add 4 tablespoons of the made green curry paste, then simmer for 15 minutes, or until fragrant. Add the palm sugar, fish sauce and makrut leaves to the pan.

Stir in the remaining coconut cream and the chicken, bamboo shoots and beans, and simmer for 15 minutes, or until the chicken is tender. Stir in the Thai basil and serve.

Lift off the thick coconut cream from the top of the tins.

Simmer the coconut cream until it 'splits' — the oil separates.

Cook the curry paste in the coconut cream until oily.

fish koftas in tomato curry sauce . . . . serves 6

KOFTAS WERE ORIGINALLY INVENTED BY THE ARABS AND HAVE PROVED TO BE IMMENSELY VERSATILE. IN THIS DISH, BOTH THE KOFTA AND THE SAUCE ARE QUITE AROMATIC; HOWEVER, THE SPICES COMPLEMENT EACH OTHER RATHER THAN COMPETE. THE SAUCE IS SLIGHTLY SWEET AND EARTHY, WHILE THE KOFTA ARE RICH AND SPICY.

koftas

skinless, firm white fish fillets	750 g (1 lb 10 oz), roughly chopped
onion	1, chopped
garlic	2–3 cloves, crushed
ginger	1 tablespoon grated
coriander (cilantro)	4 tablespoons chopped leaves
garam masala	1 teaspoon
chilli powder	1/4 teaspoon
egg	1, lightly beaten
oil	for shallow-frying

tomato curry sauce

oil	2 tablespoons
onion	1 large, finely chopped
garlic	3–4 cloves, crushed
ginger	1 tablespoon grated
ground turmeric	1 teaspoon
ground cumin	1 teaspoon
ground coriander	1 teaspoon
garam masala	1 teaspoon
chilli powder	1/4 teaspoon
tomatoes	800 g (1 lb 12 oz) tinned, crushed
coriander (cilantro)	3 tablespoons chopped leaves, plus extra sprigs, to serve

Put the fish in a food processor, or in a mortar with a pestle, and process or pound to a smooth paste. Add the onion, garlic, ginger, coriander leaves, garam masala, chilli powder and egg, and process or pound until well combined. Using wetted hands, form 1 tablespoon of the mixture into a ball. Repeat with the remaining mixture.

To make the tomato curry sauce, heat the oil in a large saucepan, add the onion, garlic and ginger, and cook, stirring frequently, over medium heat for 8 minutes, or until lightly golden.

Add the spices and cook, stirring, for 2 minutes, or until aromatic. Add the tomato and 250 ml (9 fl oz/1 cup) water, then reduce the heat and simmer, stirring frequently, for 15 minutes, or until reduced and thickened.

Meanwhile, heat the oil in a large frying pan to the depth of 2 cm (3/4 in). Add the fish koftas in 3 or 4 batches and cook for 3 minutes, or until browned all over. Drain on paper towel.

Add the koftas to the sauce and simmer over low heat for 5 minutes, or until heated through. Gently fold in the coriander, season with salt and serve garnished with coriander sprigs.

thai basil, beef and green peppercorn curry

serves 4

THERE ARE TWO INGREDIENTS IN THIS DISH THAT MAKE IT DISTINCTLY THAI (THREE IF WE INCLUDE THE CURRY PASTE). THE FIRST IS THAI BASIL, WITH ITS DISTINCTIVE PERFUME AND CLEAN FLAVOUR. THE SECOND IS PICKLED GREEN PEPPERCORNS. THEY ADD A SALTY, VINEGARY, SLIGHTLY SWEET QUALITY, WITHOUT TOO MUCH HEAT.

ginger	2 tablespoons grated
garlic	2 cloves, crushed
rump or round steak	500 g (1 lb 2 oz)
coconut cream	250 ml (9 fl oz/1 cup)
yellow curry paste	1 tablespoon, ready-made or see recipe on page 41
fish sauce	80 ml (2½ fl oz/⅓ cup)
palm sugar (jaggery)	60 g (2¼ oz/⅓ cup) shaved
lemon grass	2 stems, white part only, finely chopped
galangal	1 thick slice
makrut (kaffir lime) leaves	4
tomatoes	2, cut into 2 cm (¾ in) dice
bamboo pieces	400 g (14 oz) tinned large, drained, cut into small chunks
Thai pickled green peppercorns	25 g (1 oz), on the stem
tamarind purée	2 tablespoons
Thai basil	1 large handful, chopped

Crush the ginger and garlic to a rough pulp in a mortar with a pestle, or food processor. Cut the meat into strips 5 x 2 cm (2 x ¾ in) and 3 mm (⅛ in) thick. Toss the ginger and garlic paste together with the beef and marinate for 30 minutes.

Bring half the coconut cream to the boil in a heavy-based casserole dish over medium heat then reduce to a simmer. Stir in the yellow curry paste and cook for 3–5 minutes. Add the fish sauce and palm sugar and stir until sugar is dissolved.

Increase heat to high, add the remaining ingredients and 375 ml (13 fl oz/1½ cups) water and bring the curry to the boil then reduce to a simmer and cook uncovered for 1–1¼ hours, or until the beef is tender.

Check seasoning and correct by adding extra fish sauce or palm sugar if necessary. Stir through the remaining coconut cream and serve immediately.

Pound the ginger and garlic together to a rough pulp.

Stir in the yellow curry paste and cook until aromatic.

Add the palm sugar to the mixture and stir until dissolved.

five-spice pork curry . . . . serves 4

THIS DISH DRAWS ON VARIOUS INFLUENCES TO CREATE A SPICY, SALTY AND FRAGRANT DISH. FIVE-SPICE IS WIDELY USED IN MANY ASIAN COUNTRIES BESIDES CHINA, AND HERE IT IS MIXED WITH KECAP MANIS, A THICK, SWEET DARK SOY SAUCE FROM INDONESIA. FIVE-SPICE IS STRONGLY FLAVOURED, SO USE SPARINGLY.

pork spare ribs	500 g (1 lb 2 oz)
oil	1 1/2 tablespoons
garlic	2 cloves, crushed
fried tofu puffs	190 g (6 3/4 oz)
ginger	1 tablespoon finely chopped
five-spice	1 teaspoon
ground white pepper	1/2 teaspoon
fish sauce	3 tablespoons
kecap manis	3 tablespoons
light soy sauce	2 tablespoons
palm sugar (jaggery)	35 g (1 1/4 oz/1/4 cup) shaved
coriander (cilantro)	1 small handful leaves, chopped
snow peas (mangetout)	100 g (3 1/2 oz), thinly sliced

Cut the spare ribs into 2.5 cm (1 in) thick pieces, discarding any small pieces of bone. Put into a saucepan and cover with cold water. Bring to the boil then reduce to a simmer and cook for 5 minutes. Drain and set aside.

Heat the oil in a heavy-based saucepan over medium–high heat. Add the pork and garlic and stir until lightly browned. Add remaining ingredients except snow peas, plus 560 ml (19 1/4 fl oz/ 2 1/4 cups) water. Cover, bring to the boil then reduce to a simmer and cook, stirring occasionally, for 15–18 minutes, or until the pork is tender. Stir in the snow peas and serve.

Five-spice originated in China, though it is now used in many parts of Southeast Asia. It contains ground star anise, fennel seeds, cassia or cinnamon, Szechuan pepper and cloves. As with all spice blends, proportions vary depending on the cook, though generally the star anise dominates. In some versions, five-spice is not five at all but six- or seven-spice — ginger and/or cardamom may sneak in. This blend is pungent and quite potent, so a little goes a long way. It is used in marinades for meat, fish or poultry — its most famous use is in the marinade for Peking duck — and also with vegetables, in stir-fries and even on fruit.

three ways with tomatoes

A JUICY BURST OF RIPE TOMATO ON THE PALATE CAN BE JUST THE THING WHEN EATING A CURRY. SWEET, CLEANSING AND REFRESHING, IT IS AN IDEAL INGREDIENT FOR A RELISH. IN THE FIRST RELISH HERE IT IS COMBINED WITH LIVELY MINT AND LIME, IN THE SECOND WITH FRESH CORIANDER AND GREEN CHILLIES. INDIAN PICKLES ARE DIFFERENT CREATURES: DESIGNED TO STIMULATE THE PALATE, THEY ARE COOKED IN OIL WITH LITTLE OR NO SUGAR, AND ARE SHARP, SPICY AND STRONGLY FLAVOURED.

tomato, lime and mint relish

Peel 1 lime removing all white pith, finely dice and put into a medium non-metallic bowl with 2 diced tomatoes, 1 finely sliced spring onion (scallion), 2 tablespoons chopped mint, 1 teaspoon fish sauce, 1 teaspoon coconut vinegar (fermented coconut sap) and 1 teaspoon shaved palm sugar (jaggery). Stir to combine, and allow to sit covered in the refrigerator 30 minutes before serving. This relish goes well with spicy Thai curries. Serves 4.

tomato and coriander relish

Mix together 2 diced tomatoes, 3 finely sliced spring onions (scallions), 2 tablespoons finely chopped coriander (cilantro) leaves, 1 finely sliced green chilli, 1 tablespoon lemon juice and 1 teaspoon soft brown sugar. Season with salt and pepper and allow to sit covered in the refrigerator 30 minutes before serving. This relish goes well with Indian and Thai curries. Serves 4.

indian tomato oil pickle

Put 2 teaspoons black or brown mustard seeds and 80 ml (2$\frac{1}{2}$ fl oz/$\frac{1}{3}$ cup) cider vinegar in a small saucepan, and heat over low heat for 12 minutes, or until the seeds just start to pop. The vinegar will be nearly evaporated. Allow to cool. Put the seeds, 1 tablespoon grated ginger and 5 chopped garlic cloves in a food processor, or in a mortar with a pestle, and process or pound to a smooth paste. Heat 3 tablespoons oil in a saucepan, add 3 teaspoons ground cumin and 2 teaspoons ground turmeric and cook, stirring gently, over low heat for 4 minutes, or until fragrant. Add the mustard seed mixture, 1 teaspoon chilli powder, 1 kg (2 lb 4 oz) peeled, seeded and chopped firm, ripe tomatoes, 3 tablespoons sugar and 1 teaspoon salt. Reduce the heat and simmer, stirring occasionally, for 45 minutes, or until thick. Stir through 1 extra tablespoon of cider vinegar. Spoon into clean, warm jars, seal and cool. Refrigerate for up to 1 month. This pickle is best served with Indian curries. Serves 6.

paneer and pea curry . . . . serves 5

THIS SUBSTANTIAL YET FRAGRANT DISH IS AN EXCELLENT STARTING POINT FOR A VEGETARIAN MEAL. PANEER IS AN INDIAN COTTAGE CHEESE THAT IS MADE BY HEATING AND CURDLING MILK, THEN SEPARATING THE SOLIDS. IT SHOULD ALWAYS BE MADE FRESHLY, AS IT LASTS ONLY A FEW DAYS, THOUGH IT CAN BE BOUGHT READY-MADE.

paneer

milk	2 litres (70 fl oz/8 cups)
lemon juice	80 ml (2 1/2 fl oz/1/3 cup)
oil	for deep-frying

curry paste

onions	2 large
garlic	3 cloves
ginger	1 teaspoon grated
cumin seeds	1 teaspoon
dried red chillies	3
cardamom seeds	1 teaspoon
cloves	4
fennel seeds	1 teaspoon
cassia bark	2 pieces

peas	500 g (1 lb 2 oz)
oil	2 tablespoons
tomato passata (puréed tomatoes)	400 ml (14 fl oz)
garam masala	1 tablespoon
ground coriander	1 teaspoon
ground turmeric	1/4 teaspoon
cream (whipping)	1 tablespoon
coriander (cilantro)	leaves, to serve

Put the milk in a large saucepan, bring to the boil, stir in the lemon juice and turn off the heat. Stir the mixture for 1–2 seconds as it curdles. Put in a colander and leave for 30 minutes for the whey to drain off. Place the paneer curds on a clean, flat surface, cover with a plate, weigh down and leave for at least 4 hours.

Put all the curry paste ingredients in a food processor, or in a mortar with a pestle, and process or pound to a smooth paste.

Cut the solid paneer into 2 cm (3/4 in) cubes. Fill a deep heavy-based saucepan one-third full of oil and heat to 180°C (350°F), or until a cube of bread browns in 15 seconds. Cook the paneer in batches for 2–3 minutes, or until golden. Drain on paper towel.

Bring a saucepan of water to the boil, add the peas and cook for 3 minutes, or until tender. Drain and set aside.

Heat the oil in a large saucepan, add the curry paste and cook over medium heat for 4 minutes, or until fragrant. Add the puréed tomato, spices, cream and 125 ml (4 fl oz/1/2 cup) water. Season with salt and simmer over medium heat for 5 minutes. Add the paneer and peas and cook for 3 minutes. Garnish with coriander leaves and serve.

Strain for 30 minutes to help dry out the curds.

Deep-fry the paneer cubes in batches until golden.

kenyan coriander lamb .... serves 6

MUCH OF KENYAN CUISINE IS FAIRLY SIMPLE, SO IT IS A SURPRISE TO COME ACROSS INDIAN SPICES AND ARABIAN AND PORTUGUESE INFLUENCES IN A CURRY. BUT THE SWAHILI CUISINE OF THE KENYAN COAST IS JUST SUCH A VIBRANT FUSION, USING INTRODUCED AND LOCAL INGREDIENTS TO PRODUCE COLOURFUL AND RICHLY SPICED DISHES.

garlic	4 cloves, crushed
ginger	1 1/2 tablespoons chopped
lemon juice	2 1/2 tablespoons
lamb leg or shoulder	1 kg (2 lb 4 oz), diced
coriander seeds	1 1/2 tablespoons
black peppercorns	1/4 teaspoon
tomatoes	2, chopped
tomato paste (concentrated purée)	2 teaspoons
long green chillies	3, seeded, chopped
coriander (cilantro)	1 handful, stalks and roots, roughly chopped
oil	3 tablespoons
chicken stock	250 ml (9 fl oz/1 cup)
plain yoghurt	2 tablespoons
coriander (cilantro)	1 large handful leaves, finely chopped, to serve

Put the garlic, ginger, lemon juice and enough water to form a paste in a food processor, or in a mortar with a pestle, and process or pound to a smooth paste. Put the lamb into a non-metallic bowl, add the garlic paste, and mix well to combine. Cover and refrigerate for 2 hours.

Dry-fry the coriander seeds and peppercorns in a frying pan over medium–high heat for 2–3 minutes, or until fragrant. Allow to cool. Using a mortar with a pestle, or a spice grinder, crush or grind to a powder.

Put the ground spices, tomato, tomato paste, chillies and coriander stalks and roots in a food processor, or in a mortar with a pestle, and process or pound to a smooth paste.

Heat the oil in a heavy-based saucepan over medium–high heat. Brown the lamb in batches. When all the lamb is done, return to the pan with the tomato chilli paste, and the stock. Bring to the boil then reduce to a slow simmer, cover and cook for 1 1/2 hours, remove the lid, and cook for a further 15 minutes, or until the lamb is very tender. While cooking, skim any oil that comes to the surface and discard.

Remove from the heat and gently stir through the yoghurt, garnish with chopped coriander leaves and serve.

Process the garlic, ginger and lemon juice until smooth.

Process the spices, with the tomato and tomato paste.

Brown the lamb in batches before adding the tomato chilli paste.

spicy chicken and tomato curry.................serves 8–10

THIS RECIPE LEAVES BARELY A SPICE UNTOUCHED! CONTAINING SPICES THAT RANGE FROM HOT TO SWEET, SHARP TO GENTLY PERFUMED, THIS IS A DISH WHERE THE CHICKEN SUPPORTS THE FLAVOURINGS, NOT THE OTHER WAY ROUND. IT IS ALSO A SIMPLE DISH TO PREPARE.

oil	1 tablespoon
chickens	2 x 1.5 kg (3 lb 5 oz) jointed
onion	1, sliced
ground cloves	1/2 teaspoon
ground turmeric	1 teaspoon
garam masala	2 teaspoons
chilli powder	3 teaspoons
cardamom pods	3
garlic	3 cloves, crushed
ginger	1 tablespoon grated
poppy seeds	1 tablespoon
fennel seeds	2 teaspoons
coconut milk	250 ml (9 fl oz/1 cup)
star anise	1
cinnamon stick	1
tomatoes	4 large, roughly chopped
lime juice	2 tablespoons

Heat the oil in a large frying pan over medium heat, add the chicken in batches and cook for 5–10 minutes, or until browned, then transfer to a large saucepan.

Add the onion to the frying pan and cook, stirring, for 10–12 minutes, or until golden. Stir in the ground cloves, turmeric, garam masala and chilli powder, and cook, stirring, for 1 minute, then add to the chicken.

Lightly crush the cardamom pods with the flat side of a heavy knife. Remove the seeds, discarding the pods. Put the seeds and the garlic, ginger, poppy seeds, fennel seeds and 2 tablespoons of the coconut milk in a food processor, or in a mortar with a pestle, and process or pound to a smooth paste. Add the spice mixture, remaining coconut milk, star anise, cinnamon stick, tomato and 3 tablespoons water to the chicken.

Simmer, covered, for 45 minutes, or until the chicken is tender. Remove the chicken, cover and keep warm. Bring the cooking liquid to the boil and boil for 20–25 minutes, or until reduced by half. Put the chicken on a serving plate, mix the lime juice with the cooking liquid and pour over the chicken.

Brown the chicken in the frying pan in batches.

Fry the onions until golden before adding the spices.

thai green curry with fish balls ....serves 4

A LONG-TIME THAI FAVOURITE, THIS DISH FEATURES FISH BALLS OR DUMPLINGS RATHER THAN PIECES OF FISH (HOWEVER, SLICES OF FISH CAN ALSO BE USED). THAI EGGPLANTS (AUBERGINES), GALANGAL AND TANGY MAKRUT (KAFFIR LIME) LEAVES ADD DEPTH TO THE SPICY CURRY BASE, WHILE THE POUNDED FISH PROVIDES TEXTURE.

skinless, firm white fish fillets	350 g (12 oz), roughly cut into pieces
coconut cream	3 tablespoons
green curry paste	2 tablespoons, ready-made or see recipe on page 130
coconut milk	440 ml (15¼ fl oz/1¾ cups) (do not shake the tin), plus extra for topping
Thai apple eggplants (aubergines)	175 g (6 oz), quartered
pea eggplants (aubergines)	175 g (6 oz)
fish sauce	2 tablespoons
palm sugar (jaggery)	2 tablespoons shaved
galangal	50 g (1¾ oz), finely sliced
makrut (kaffir lime) leaves	3, torn in half
holy basil	1 handful, to serve
long red chilli	½, seeded, finely sliced, to serve

Put the fish fillets in a food processor, or in a mortar with a pestle, and process or pound to a smooth paste.

Put the thick coconut cream from the top of the tin in a saucepan, bring to a rapid simmer over medium heat, stirring occasionally, and cook for 5–10 minutes, or until the mixture 'splits' (the oil starts to separate). Add the curry paste and cook for 5 minutes, or until fragrant. Add the remaining coconut milk and mix well.

Use a spoon or your wet hands to shape the fish paste into small balls, about 2 cm (¾ in) across, and drop them into the coconut milk. Add the eggplants, fish sauce and sugar and cook for 12–15 minutes, stirring occasionally, or until the fish and eggplants are cooked.

Stir in the galangal and makrut leaves. Taste, then adjust the seasoning if necessary. Spoon into a serving bowl and sprinkle with extra coconut milk, basil leaves and sliced chilli.

Process the skinless fish fillets to a smooth paste.

Stir the paste into the coconut cream and cook until fragrant.

Shape the fish paste into small balls with wet hands.

prawns with thai basil . . . . serves 4

THIS FRAGRANT AND TASTY CURRY COULDN'T BE EASIER TO MAKE. ONCE THE PRAWNS ARE PREPARED, THE COOKING TAKES ONLY MINUTES. THE SAUCE SHOULD BE THICK, HOT AND SWEET, SO MAKE SURE YOUR SAUCEPAN OR WOK IS HOT ENOUGH TO REDUCE THE COCONUT MILK AS SOON AS IT IS ADDED.

curry paste

dried long red chillies	2
lemon grass	2 stems, white part only, finely sliced
galangal	2.5 cm (1 in) piece, finely sliced
garlic	5 cloves, crushed
red Asian shallots	4, finely chopped
coriander (cilantro)	6 roots, finely chopped
shrimp paste	1 teaspoon
ground cumin	1 teaspoon
unsalted peanuts	3 tablespoons, chopped
raw prawns (shrimp)	600 g (1 lb 5 oz), peeled, deveined, tails intact
oil	2 tablespoons
coconut milk	185 ml (6 fl oz/3/4 cup)
fish sauce	2 teaspoons
palm sugar (jaggery)	2 teaspoons shaved
Thai basil leaves	1 handful, to serve

Soak the chillies in boiling water for 5 minutes, or until soft. Remove the seeds and stems and chop. Put the chillies and the remaining curry paste ingredients in a food processor, or in a mortar with a pestle, and process or pound to a smooth paste.

Cut each prawn along the back so it opens like a butterfly (leave each prawn joined along the base and at the tail). Heat the oil in a saucepan or wok and stir-fry 2 tablespoons of the curry paste over a medium heat for 2 minutes, or until fragrant.

Add the coconut milk, fish sauce and palm sugar and cook for a few seconds. Add the prawns and cook for a few minutes or until cooked through. Taste, then adjust the seasoning if necessary. Serve garnished with Thai basil.

There are three main types of basil used in Thai cuisine. The most important by far is Thai basil, also known as Thai sweet basil. This variety has purplish stems, lush, deep green leaves and an aniseed aroma and flavour. It is added liberally to a wide range of dishes. Next up is holy basil, which is available in two types: red- and white-stemmed. Highly perfumed and with a peppery taste, holy basil is always cooked to release its flavour. The final type is lemon basil, also called mint basil. As its name suggests, it has a fresh, tangy scent and flavour and is delicious with fish, poultry and sweet drinks and desserts.

lamb and spinach curry . . . . serves 6

THIS IS A RICHLY FLAVOURED, TRADITIONAL DISH FROM THE PUNJAB REGION OF NORTHERN INDIA. IT IS COOKED UNTIL THE SAUCE IS VERY THICK AND FAIRLY DRY AND THE DISTINCTIVE FLAVOURS OF THE LAMB AND ENGLISH SPINACH HAVE BLENDED TO FORM A SMOOTH, UNIFIED WHOLE. IT CAN BE SERVED WITH EITHER RICE OR BREADS.

coriander seeds	2 teaspoons
cumin seeds	1½ teaspoons
oil	3 tablespoons
leg or shoulder of lamb	1 kg (2 lb 4 oz) boneless, cut into 2.5 cm (1 in) cubes
onions	4, finely chopped
cloves	6
cardamom pods	6
cinnamon stick	1
black peppercorns	10
Indian bay (cassia) leaves	4
garam masala	3 teaspoons
ground turmeric	¼ teaspoon
paprika	1 teaspoon
ginger	7 cm (2¾ in) piece, grated
garlic cloves	4, crushed
Greek-style yoghurt	185 g (6½ oz/¾ cup)
amaranth or English spinach leaves	450 g (1 lb), roughly chopped

Dry-fry the coriander and cumin seeds in a frying pan over medium–high heat for 2–3 minutes, or until fragrant. Allow to cool. Using a mortar with a pestle, or a spice grinder, crush or grind to a powder.

Heat the oil in a flameproof casserole dish over low heat and fry a few pieces of meat at a time until browned. Remove from the dish. Add more oil to the dish, if necessary, and fry the onion, cloves, cardamom pods, cinnamon stick, peppercorns and bay leaves until the onion is lightly browned. Add the cumin and coriander, garam masala, turmeric and paprika and fry for 30 seconds.

Add the meat, ginger, garlic, yoghurt and 425 ml (15 fl oz) water and bring to the boil. Reduce the heat to a simmer, cover and cook for 1½–2 hours, or until the meat is very tender. At this stage, most of the water should have evaporated. If it hasn't, remove the lid, increase the heat and cook until the moisture has evaporated.

Cook the spinach briefly in a little simmering water until it is just wilted, then refresh in cold water. Drain thoroughly, then finely chop. Squeeze out any extra water in the spinach. Add the spinach to the lamb and cook for 3 minutes, or until the spinach and lamb are well mixed and any extra liquid has evaporated.

green herb pork curry .... serves 6

A GENEROUS USE OF CORIANDER (CILANTRO) AND DILL, MIXED WITH YOGHURT AND ADDED AT THE LAST MINUTE TO THE CURRY, GIVES THIS DISH A BURST OF FRESH HERB FLAVOUR. BALANCING THIS ARE THE WARMER, ROUNDER, ROASTED AROMAS OF FENNEL AND CORIANDER SEEDS.

coriander seeds	2 teaspoons
fennel seeds	2 teaspoons
ground white pepper	1/4 teaspoon
ginger	1 1/2 tablespoons grated
garlic	6 cloves, crushed
onions	2, chopped
oil	3 tablespoons
pork shoulder	1 kg (2 lb 4 oz), cut into 2 cm (3/4 in) dice
chicken stock	250 ml (9 fl oz/1 cup)
plain yoghurt	125 g (4 1/2 oz/1/2 cup)
coriander (cilantro)	1 large handful leaves, roughly chopped
dill	1 large handful, roughly chopped

Dry-fry the coriander and fennel seeds in a frying pan over medium–high heat for 2–3 minutes, or until fragrant. Allow to cool. Using a mortar with a pestle, or a spice grinder, crush or grind to a powder.

Put the ground coriander and fennel seeds along with the pepper, ginger, garlic and onion in a food processor, or in a mortar with a pestle, and process or pound to a smooth paste. Add a little water if it is too thick.

Heat 2 tablespoons of the oil in a heavy-based saucepan over high heat, and brown the pork in batches. Set aside. Reduce heat to low then add the remaining oil, and cook the spice and onion paste, stirring constantly, for 5–8 minutes. Add the pork back to the pan, and stir to coat with the paste. Add the chicken stock, increase heat to high and bring to the boil then reduce to a very slow simmer, cover and cook for 2–2 1/2 hours, or until the pork is very tender. While cooking, stir occasionally and skim any oil that comes to the surface and discard.

Put the yoghurt, chopped coriander, dill and 3 tablespoons of the cooking liquid from the pork into a jug or bowl and blend with a stick blender until smooth, then add back into the pork. Remove from heat, season well to taste and serve.

Process or pound the onion mixture to a smooth paste.

Stir the pork into the paste mixture, coating well.

Blend the yoghurt, herbs and cooking liquid until smooth.

chicken masala .... serves 4

MASALA SIMPLY MEANS 'MIXTURE OF SPICES', A CATCH-ALL WORD THAT COULD BE USED WITH JUST ABOUT ANY CURRY. IN THIS CASE, THE MIXTURE IS AROMATIC BUT ONLY MODERATELY SPICY, GIVING THE DISH A SUBTLE FLAVOUR. THE COMBINATION OF TOMATOES AND GINGER ADDS A DELICIOUS EXTRA FLAVOURING TO THE SPICES.

chicken thigh fillets or chicken pieces	1.5 kg (3 lb 5 oz), skinless
ground cumin	2 teaspoons
ground coriander	2 teaspoons
garam masala	1½ teaspoons
ground turmeric	¼ teaspoon
onions	2, finely chopped
garlic	4 cloves, roughly chopped
ginger	5 cm (2 in) piece, roughly chopped
tomatoes	2 ripe, chopped
ghee or oil	3 tablespoons
cloves	5
cardamom pods	8, bruised
cinnamon stick	1
curry leaves	10
Greek-style yoghurt	160 g (5¾ oz/⅔ cup)

Trim off any excess fat from the chicken. Mix the cumin, coriander, garam masala and turmeric together and rub it into the chicken.

Put half the onion with the garlic, ginger and chopped tomato in a food processor, or in a mortar with a pestle, and process or pound to a smooth paste.

Heat the ghee or oil in a casserole dish over low heat, add the remaining onion, cloves, cardamom, cinnamon and curry leaves and fry until the onion is golden brown. Add the tomato and onion paste and stir for 5 minutes. Season with salt, to taste. Add the yoghurt and whisk until smooth, then add the spiced chicken. Toss pieces through and bring slowly to the boil.

Reduce the heat, cover and simmer for 50 minutes or until the oil separates from the sauce. Stir the ingredients occasionally to prevent the chicken from sticking. If the sauce is too thin, simmer for a couple of minutes with the lid off.

Cinnamon is familiar to us all as quills of delicate, tightly rolled, light brown layers of paper-thin bark. It is indigenous to Sri Lanka, and the world's best still comes from there. As with many spices, early traders invented fanciful tales to hide its origins and many struggles have been waged over its control. In its homeland, only a caste known as the Chalais could harvest and peel the spice. Today, we can easily buy the quills, but its sweet, inviting fragrance and taste can still conjure up an exotic past. Cinnamon is used in dishes ranging from milk puddings to pickles, and is essential in spice blends such as garam masala.

softly sweet

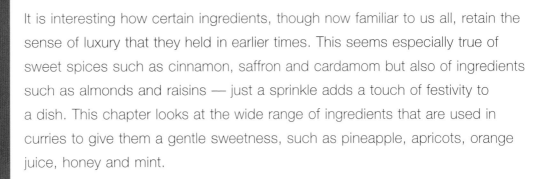

It is interesting how certain ingredients, though now familiar to us all, retain the sense of luxury that they held in earlier times. This seems especially true of sweet spices such as cinnamon, saffron and cardamom but also of ingredients such as almonds and raisins — just a sprinkle adds a touch of festivity to a dish. This chapter looks at the wide range of ingredients that are used in curries to give them a gentle sweetness, such as pineapple, apricots, orange juice, honey and mint.

Many of the sweet flavours in the following dishes come from introduced ingredients, and it is a testament to the versatility of curries that they can absorb new ingredients and very successfully make them their own. For example, the chilli, native to Central America, could not be more at home in the curries of India and Southeast Asia. But this is true also of perfumed lychees from China, sweet almonds from Persia and juicy tomatoes from South America. Barbecue duck curry with lychees has two of China's most famous ingredients, here seamlessly blended with classic curry spices such as cumin, paprika, turmeric and ground coriander, as well as the ever-present coconut cream, fish sauce and palm sugar. Minted lamb curry transfers the classic combination of fresh, sweet mint and lamb to the world of spicy curries, complementing the fresh herb taste with green chillies, tart lemon juice and sharp cayenne pepper and turmeric.

Sweet ingredients also provide the perfect opportunity for including robust flavours, such as duck and pork, but also seasonings like Indonesia's hot and spicy sambal oelek and fruit such as green bananas. As when blending hot and sour ingredients, sweet and robust flavours are used to complement each other, not compete. An Indian pork, honey and almond curry included here also contains fresh herbs, citrus zest, spices and yoghurt, all brought magically together through slow, gentle cooking. Snapper with green bananas and mango is another excellent, delicious example of the art of balance that is so central to all curries. The starchy bananas provide texture and act as a thickening agent, the mango contributes a lovely summery sweetness and the fish just absorbs it all, supported by a spicy yellow curry paste and rich coconut cream base. This chapter may appear less traditional than others in this book but it still follows the principles of curry making that make these dishes so popular the world over.

barbecue duck curry with lychees .... serves 4

THIS COLOURFUL CURRY FEATURES THE DELICATE APPEAL OF LYCHEES. NATIVE TO CHINA BUT NOW GROWN IN SOUTHEAST ASIA AND INDIA, LYCHEES HAVE A CREAMY, SWEET FLESH AND GENTLE PERFUME. THE SPICE PASTE IS EARTHY AND PEPPERY, RATHER THAN HOT, AND BALANCES WELL WITH THE RICH-TASTING MEAT AND COCONUT.

curry paste

white peppercorns	1 teaspoon
shrimp paste	1 teaspoon
long red chillies	3, seeded
red onion	1, roughly chopped
garlic	2 cloves
lemon grass	2 stems, white part only, thinly sliced
ginger	5 cm (2 in) piece
coriander (cilantro)	3 roots
makrut (kaffir lime) leaves	5
oil	2 tablespoons
ground coriander	2 teaspoons
ground cumin	1 teaspoon
paprika	1 teaspoon
ground turmeric	1 teaspoon

Chinese barbecue duck	1
coconut cream	400 ml (14 fl oz)
palm sugar (jaggery)	1 tablespoon shaved
fish sauce	2 tablespoons
galangal	1 thick slice
straw mushrooms	240 g (8½ oz) tinned, drained
lychees	400 g (14 oz) tinned, cut in half, (reserve 60 ml/2 fl oz/¼ cup syrup)
cherry tomatoes	250 g (9 oz)
Thai basil	1 handful, chopped
coriander (cilantro)	1 handful leaves, chopped

Dry-fry the peppercorns and the shrimp paste wrapped in some foil in a frying pan over medium–high heat for 2–3 minutes, or until fragrant. Allow to cool. Using a mortar with a pestle, or a spice grinder, crush or grind the peppercorns to a powder. Put the crushed peppercorns and the shrimp with the remaining curry paste ingredients in a food processor, or in a mortar with a pestle, and process or pound to a smooth paste.

Remove the duck meat from the bones and chop into bite-sized pieces. Put the thick coconut cream from the top of the tin in a saucepan, bring to a rapid simmer over medium heat, stirring occasionally, and cook for 5–10 minutes, or until the mixture 'splits' (the oil starts to separate). Add half the curry paste, palm sugar and fish sauce and stir until the palm sugar is dissolved. Add the duck, galangal, straw mushrooms, lychees, reserved lychee syrup and remaining coconut cream. Bring to the boil then reduce to a simmer and cook for 15–20 minutes, or until the duck is tender.

Add the cherry tomatoes, basil and coriander. Season to taste. Serve when the cherry tomatoes are slightly softened.

Note: When in season, you can use fresh lychees, which will be sweeter and juicier than the tinned variety so you won't need the added syrup.

Process all the curry paste ingredients until smooth.

Remove the duck meat from the bones and chop.

chicken, almond and raisin curry .... serves 6

WHILE THE CHICKEN COOKS, YOU WILL BE ABLE TO SAVOUR THE WONDERFUL AROMAS COMING FROM THIS SWEETLY SPICED CURRY. THE DISH FEATURES RELATIVELY FEW SPICES, BUT THEY ARE IN PERFECT HARMONY WITH EACH OTHER: CLOVES AND GINGER PROVIDE SHARPNESS, WHILE THE ALMONDS AND RAISINS ADD A TOUCH OF LUXURY.

cardamom pods	6
cloves	6
cumin seeds	1 teaspoon
cayenne pepper	1/2 teaspoon
ghee or oil	2 tablespoons
chicken thigh fillets	1 kg (2 lb 4 oz), cut into 3 cm (1 1/4 in) cubes
onion	1, finely chopped
garlic	3 cloves, crushed
ginger	1 1/2 tablespoons finely grated
cinnamon sticks	2
bay leaves	2
blanched almonds	50 g (1 3/4 oz/1/3 cup), lightly toasted
raisins	40 g (1 1/2 oz/1/3 cup)
plain yoghurt	250 g (9 oz/1 cup)
chicken stock	125 ml (4 fl oz/1/2 cup)

Lightly crush the cardamom pods with the flat side of a heavy knife. Remove the seeds, discarding the pods. Dry-fry the seeds along with the cloves, cumin seeds and cayenne pepper in a frying pan over medium–high heat for 2–3 minutes, or until fragrant. Allow to cool. Using a mortar with a pestle, or a spice grinder, crush or grind to a powder.

In a large heavy-based frying pan, heat the ghee or oil over medium–high heat. Brown the chicken in batches and set aside. In the same pan, cook the onion, garlic and ginger over low heat for 5–8 minutes until softened. Add the ground spice mix, cinnamon sticks and bay leaves, and cook, stirring constantly, for 5 minutes. Put the almonds, raisins and chicken back into the pan. Add the yoghurt a spoonful at a time, stirring to incorporate it into the dish. Add the chicken stock, reduce the heat to low, cover and cook for 40 minutes, or until the chicken is tender. While cooking, skim any oil that comes to the surface and discard. Season well and serve.

First introduced to India by the Persian Moguls, almonds remain a highly valued ingredient. Fragrant and creamy, they are used in Indian drinks and desserts, including the famous kulfi, and coconut- or yoghurt-based curries. The almond tree is suited to Mediterranean-style climates, so is grown only as far east as Kashmir, contributing to its allure. Almonds are available whole with skins on or blanched; chopped or slivered; flaked; and ground. Use only blanched nuts in curries: to blanch, pour boiling water over and stand for 2 minutes. Drain and slip off the skins. To toast, spread the nuts on a baking tray and cook at 180°C (350°F/Gas 4) for 8–10 minutes.

indian pork, honey and almond curry

THIS UNUSUAL CURRY BLENDS AROMATIC CINNAMON AND CARDAMOM WITH SWEET HONEY AND ALMONDS, FRAGRANT CITRUS AND THE FRESH LIVELINESS OF PARSLEY AND CORIANDER (CILANTRO). PORK IS THE PERFECT CHOICE FOR THIS MIX OF AROMAS AND FLAVOURS, COMPLEMENTING RATHER THAN BEING SWAMPED BY THEM.

cinnamon stick	1
cardamom pods	3
boneless pork shoulder	750 g (1 lb 10 oz)
oil	1 tablespoon
honey	2 tablespoons
garlic	3 cloves, crushed
onions	2, chopped
chicken stock	150 ml (5 fl oz)
ground turmeric	1 teaspoon
ground black pepper	1/2 teaspoon
lemon zest	1 teaspoon grated
orange zest	1 teaspoon grated
plain yoghurt	250 g (9 oz/1 cup)
slivered almonds	30 g (1 oz/1/4 cup), toasted
coriander (cilantro)	1 small handful leaves, chopped
flat-leaf (Italian) parsley	1 small handful, chopped

Dry-fry the cinnamon and cardamom in a frying pan over medium–high heat for 2–3 minutes, or until fragrant. Allow to cool. Using a mortar with a pestle, or a spice grinder, crush or grind to a powder.

Cut the pork into 2 cm (3/4 in) cubes. Heat the oil and honey in a heavy-based saucepan over medium heat. Add the cubed pork, garlic and onion and cook for 8–10 minutes, or until onion is translucent and pork light golden. Add 200 ml (7 fl oz) water and the chicken stock, bring to the boil then reduce to a simmer, cover and cook, stirring occasionally, for 1 hour 15 minutes, or until the pork is tender.

Uncover and bring to a rapid simmer for 10 minutes, or until most of the liquid is absorbed. Add the crushed spices, turmeric, pepper, 1 teaspoon salt and the citrus zest and simmer for a further 3–4 minutes. To serve, gently reheat, stirring in the yoghurt, almonds, chopped coriander and flat-leaf parsley.

Cut the boneless pork shoulder fillet into neat cubes.

Sauté the pork for 8–10 minutes, or until it becomes lightly golden.

Stir in the spices, salt and grated citrus zest and simmer.

indonesian pumpkin and spinach curry..serves 6

THIS CURRY CONTAINS SOME OF THE CLASSIC INGREDIENTS OF INDONESIAN COOKING, INCLUDING CANDLENUTS, SHALLOTS, GALANGAL AND SAMBAL OELEK. *SAMBAL* MEANS HOT AND SPICY — WHICH GIVES YOU AN IDEA OF THE DISH'S TASTE. THIS PARTICULAR SAMBAL IS AN UNCOOKED MIXTURE OF CHILLIES, SALT AND VINEGAR OR CITRUS.

curry paste

candlenuts	3
raw peanuts	1 tablespoon
red Asian shallots	3, chopped
garlic	2 cloves
sambal oelek	2–3 teaspoons
ground turmeric	1/4 teaspoon
galangal	1 teaspoon grated
oil	2 tablespoons
onion	1, finely chopped
butternut pumpkin (squash)	600 g (1 lb 5 oz), cut into 2 cm (3/4 in) cubes
vegetable stock	125 ml (4 fl oz/1/2 cup) (or as required)
English spinach	350 g (12 oz), roughly chopped
coconut cream	400 ml (14 fl oz)
sugar	1/4 teaspoon

Put all the curry paste ingredients in a food processor, or in a mortar with a pestle, and process or pound to a smooth paste.

Heat the oil in a large saucepan, add the curry paste and cook, stirring, over low heat for 3–5 minutes, or until fragrant. Add the onion and cook for a further 5 minutes, or until softened.

Add the pumpkin and half the vegetable stock and cook, covered, for 10 minutes, or until pumpkin is almost cooked through. Add more stock, if required. Add the spinach, coconut cream and sugar, and season with salt. Bring to the boil, stirring constantly, then reduce the heat and simmer for 3–5 minutes, or until the spinach is cooked and the sauce has thickened slightly. Serve immediately.

Process all the paste ingredients to form a smooth paste.

Stir the onion into the paste and cook until softened.

Add the pumpkin with the stock and cook until almost tender.

minced lamb with orange . . . . serves 6

THERE IS PROBABLY NO MEAT MORE VERSATILE THAN LAMB. THIS NON-TRADITIONAL CURRY BLENDS AROMATIC
GROUND SPICES WITH THE SWEETNESS OF ORANGE JUICE AND THE CLEANSING FRESHNESS OF GREEN CHILLIES
AND MINT. IT IS A THICK, WET CURRY, IDEAL FOR SERVING WITH BREAD FOR MOPPING UP ANY LEFTOVERS.

oil	3 tablespoons
onions	2, finely diced
garlic	4 cloves, crushed
ginger	3 teaspoons finely grated
ground cumin	2 teaspoons
ground coriander	2 teaspoons
ground turmeric	1/2 teaspoon
cayenne pepper	1/2 teaspoon
garam masala	1 teaspoon
minced (ground) lamb	1 kg (2 lb 4 oz)
plain yoghurt	90 g (3 1/4 oz/1/3 cup)
orange juice	250 ml (9 fl oz/1 cup)
orange zest	2 teaspoons
bay leaf	1
long green chilli	1, seeded, finely sliced
coriander (cilantro)	1 handful leaves, roughly chopped
mint	1 handful, roughly chopped

Heat the oil in a large heavy-based frying pan over medium heat. Add the onions, garlic, and ginger and sauté for 5 minutes. Add the cumin, coriander, turmeric, cayenne pepper and garam masala, and cook for a further 5 minutes.

Increase the heat to high, add the lamb mince, and cook, stirring constantly to break the meat up. Add the yoghurt, a tablespoon at a time, stirring so that it combines well. Add the orange juice, zest, and bay leaf.

Bring to the boil then reduce to a simmer, cover and cook for 45 minutes, or until tender. While cooking, skim any oil that comes to the surface and discard. Season well to taste then stir through the green chilli, coriander and mint before serving.

Native to southern Europe and the Mediterranean, coriander (cilantro) is nevertheless an essential element in curries. Fresh and dried coriander are quite different, and of the fresh plant, the leaves, stem and root can all be used. The roots are used in curry pastes and sauces: the stems when a strong coriander flavour is needed, and the leaves are added at the end of cooking, for flavouring and to garnish. Fresh coriander is fragrant with a gingery edge, while the dried seeds have a sweeter, slightly peppery aroma. The flavour and aroma of the whole seeds are enhanced if they are lightly dry-fried before crushing.

three ways with bread

A CURRY SERVED ON ITS OWN IS NO CURRY AT ALL. RICE, SIDE DISHES OF RAITAS OR CHUTNEYS AND BREADS SUCH AS NAAN ARE WHAT MAKES THEM COMPLETE. FURTHERMORE, IT'S A RARE CURRY THAT DOES NOT HAPPILY LEND ITSELF TO BEING SCOOPED UP WITH SOME BREAD. HERE ARE THREE CLASSIC CHOICES: DRY, UNLEAVENED ROTIS AND CHAPATIS, THE BASIC EVERYDAY BREADS OF INDIA; AND SOFT, OVEN-BAKED NAAN, WHICH ARE LEAVENED WITH A STARTER TO GIVE THEM THEIR PUFFED APPEARANCE.

roti

Sift 375 g (13 oz/3 cups) roti or plain (all-purpose) flour into a large mixing bowl with 1 teaspoon salt. Rub in 2 tablespoons softened ghee or oil with your fingertips. Add 1 lightly beaten egg and 250 ml (9 fl oz/1 cup) warm water, and mix together with a flat-bladed knife to form a moist dough. Turn out on to a well-floured surface and knead for 10 minutes, or until you have a soft dough. Sprinkle with more flour as necessary. Form the dough into a ball and brush with oil. Place in a bowl, cover and rest for 2 hours. Working on a lightly-floured bench top, divide the dough into 12 pieces and roll into even-sized balls. Take one ball and, working with a little oil on your fingertips, hold the ball in the air and work around the edge pulling out the dough until a 2 mm x 15 cm (1/16 x 6 in) round is formed. Lay on a lightly-floured surface and cover with plastic wrap so that it doesn't dry out. Repeat the process with the remaining balls. Heat a large frying pan over high heat and brush it with ghee or oil. Carefully place one roti in the frying pan, brush with some extra beaten egg and cook for 1 minute, or until the underside is golden. Slide onto a plate and brush the pan with some more ghee or oil. Cook the other side of the roti for 50–60 seconds, or until golden. Remove from the pan and cover to keep warm. Cook the remaining rotis in the same way. Makes 12.

chapati

Put 280 g (10 oz/2 1/4 cups) atta (chapati) flour in a large bowl with a pinch of salt. Slowly add 250 ml (9 fl oz/1 cup) water, or enough to form a firm dough. Put on a lightly floured surface and knead until smooth. Cover with plastic wrap and leave for 50 minutes. Divide into 14 portions and roll into 14 cm (5 1/2 in) circles. Heat a frying pan over medium heat and brush with melted ghee or oil. Cook the chapatis one at a time, flattening the surface, for 2–3 minutes on each side, or until golden brown and bubbles appear. Makes 14.

naan

Preheat the oven to 200°C (400°F/Gas 6). Lightly grease two 28 x 32 cm (11 1/4 x 12 3/4 in) baking trays. Sift together 500 g (1 lb 2 oz/ 4 cups) plain (all-purpose) flour, 1 teaspoon baking powder, 1/2 teaspoon bicarbonate of soda (baking soda) and 1 teaspoon salt. Mix in 1 beaten egg, 1 tablespoon melted ghee or butter, 125 g (4 1/2 oz/1/2 cup) plain yoghurt and gradually add enough milk to form a soft dough — about 250 ml (9 fl oz/1 cup). Cover with a damp cloth and leave in a warm place for 2 hours. Knead the dough on a well-floured surface for 2–3 minutes, or until smooth. Divide into 8 portions and roll each one into an oval 15 cm (6 in) long. Brush with water and place, wet side down, on the prepared baking trays. Brush with melted ghee or butter and bake for 8–10 minutes, or until golden brown. To make garlic naan, crush 6 garlic cloves and sprinkle evenly over the dough prior to baking. Makes 8.

snapper with green bananas and mango

THIS IMPRESSIVE-LOOKING CURRY IS RICHLY FLAVOURED WITH SPICES, HERBS AND TROPICAL FRUIT. ROBUST FRUIT LIKE GREEN BANANA MAKES AN INTERESTING TEXTURAL ADDITION TO CURRIES — THE BANANA IS VERY STARCHY, MORE LIKE A VEGETABLE THAN A FRUIT, AND WILL HELP TO THICKEN THE CURRY.

curry paste

coriander seeds	3 teaspoons
cumin seeds	1 teaspoon
dried long red chillies	2–3
lemon grass	2 stems, white part only, finely sliced
red Asian shallots	3, finely chopped
garlic	2 cloves, crushed
ground turmeric	1 teaspoon
shrimp paste	1 teaspoon

ground turmeric	1 teaspoon
green banana or plantain	1 small, thinly sliced
coconut cream	3 tablespoons
fish sauce	1 tablespoon
palm sugar (jaggery)	1 teaspoon shaved
snapper or other skinless, firm white fish fillets	400 g (14 oz), cut into large cubes
coconut milk	315 ml (10¾ fl oz/1¼ cups)
mango	1 small, just ripe, cut into thin slices
long green chilli	1, finely sliced
Thai basil leaves	12

Dry-fry the coriander and cumin seeds in a frying pan over medium–high heat for 2–3 minutes, or until fragrant. Allow to cool. Using a mortar with a pestle, or a spice grinder, crush or grind to a powder.

Soak the chillies in boiling water for 5 minutes, or until soft. Remove the stem and seeds, then chop. Put the chillies, the ground coriander and cumin seeds with the remaining curry paste ingredients in a food processor, or in a mortar with a pestle, and process or pound to a smooth paste. Add a little oil if it is too thick.

Bring a small saucepan of water to the boil. Add 1 teaspoon salt, turmeric and banana slices and simmer for 10 minutes, then drain.

Put the coconut cream in a saucepan, bring to a rapid simmer over medium heat, stirring occasionally, and cook for 5–10 minutes, or until the mixture 'splits' (the oil starts to separate). Add 2 tablespoons of the made curry paste, stir well to combine and cook until fragrant. Add the fish sauce and sugar and cook for another 2 minutes or until the mixture begins to darken.

Add the fish pieces and stir well to coat the fish in the curry mixture. Slowly add the coconut milk until it has all been incorporated.

Add the banana, mango, green chilli and the basil leaves to the pan and gently stir to combine all the ingredients. Cook for a further 1–2 minutes, then serve.

minted lamb curry . . . . serves 6

WONDERFULLY FRESH TASTING, MINT IS MORE OFTEN ASSOCIATED WITH CHUTNEYS, SALADS AND TEAS THAN CURRIES, BUT THIS SIMPLE DISH PROVES THAT IT CAN WORK WELL IN THIS ARENA, TOO. HERE, IT IS COMBINED WITH CORIANDER (CILANTRO), GREEN CHILLIES AND LEMON JUICE, CREATING A REFRESHING CURRY.

lamb shoulder	1 kg (2 lb 4 oz), cut into 2 cm (3/4 in) dice
onions	4, finely sliced
garlic	3 cloves, crushed
ginger	3 teaspoons finely chopped
cayenne pepper	1/2 teaspoon
turmeric	1 teaspoon
chicken stock	125 ml (4 fl oz/1/2 cup)
coriander (cilantro)	1 handful leaves and stalks
mint	1 handful
long green chillies	3
lemon juice	3 tablespoons
sugar	1 teaspoon

Put the lamb, onions, garlic, ginger, cayenne, turmeric, and chicken stock in a heavy-based saucepan over medium heat. Bring to a simmer, reduce to low heat, cover and cook for 2 hours. Skim the surface to remove any oil and discard.

Put the coriander leaves and stalks, mint leaves, green chillies, lemon juice and 2 tablespoons of cooking liquid from the curry in a food processor, or in a mortar with a pestle, and process or pound to a smooth consistency. Pour into the lamb mixture, put back on the heat until it just comes back up to a simmer. Add the sugar, season well to taste and serve.

Throughout its culinary history, mint has been used with remarkable consistency — that is, with meat, particularly lamb, in drinks and in sauces and pickles. In India and Southeast Asia, it appears in cold and hot drinks, salads, chutneys, raitas and desserts — as well as the occasional curry. In these countries, where much of the food is hot and spicy, mint is greatly valued for its cooling properties and sweet, light flavour. There are many local varieties of mint, but common garden mint is a fine substitute. Buy fresh leaves and store for up to a week in the refrigerator, or tightly seal in a bag and freeze.

vietnamese mild chicken curry .... serves 6

VIETNAMESE FOOD IS AN INTRIGUING MIX OF INDIGENOUS, FRENCH AND ASIAN INFLUENCES. CURRIES ARE FOUND MAINLY IN THE TROPICAL SOUTHERN AREAS OF THE COUNTRY, AND THOUGH OFTEN SHOWING LINKS WITH INDIAN COOKING, ARE NOT AS RICH OR AS SPICY AS THOSE FROM INDIA OR THAILAND.

chicken leg quarters	4 large
Indian curry powder	1 tablespoon
caster (superfine) sugar	1 teaspoon
oil	80 ml (2½ fl oz/⅓ cup)
sweet potato	500 g (1 lb 2 oz), cut into 3 cm (1¼ in) cubes
onion	1 large, cut into thin wedges
garlic	4 cloves, crushed
lemon grass	1 stem, white part only, finely chopped
bay leaves	2
carrot	1 large, cut into 1 cm (½ in) pieces on the diagonal
coconut milk	400 ml (14 fl oz)
Thai basil	to serve

Remove the skin and any excess fat from the chicken. Pat dry with paper towel and cut each quarter into 3 even pieces. Put the curry powder, sugar, ½ teaspoon black pepper and 2 teaspoons salt in a bowl, and mix well. Rub the curry mixture into the chicken pieces. Put the chicken pieces on a plate, cover with plastic wrap and refrigerate overnight.

Heat the oil in a large saucepan. Add the sweet potato and cook over medium heat for 3 minutes, or until lightly golden. Remove with a slotted spoon.

Remove all but 2 tablespoons of the oil from the pan. Add the onion and cook, stirring, for 5 minutes. Add the garlic, lemon grass and bay leaves, and cook for 2 minutes.

Add the chicken and cook, stirring, over medium heat for 5 minutes, or until well coated in the mixture and starting to change colour. Add 250 ml (9 fl oz/1 cup) water and simmer, covered, stirring occasionally, for 20 minutes.

Stir in the carrot, sweet potato and coconut milk, and simmer, uncovered, stirring occasionally, for 30 minutes, or until the chicken is cooked and tender. Be careful not to break up the sweet potato cubes. Serve topped with Thai basil.

Remove the skin and any excess fat from the chicken.

Sauté the sweet potato until lightly golden.

Pour in the coconut milk and simmer until the chicken is tender.

thai sweet pork and pineapple curry..serves 4

THIS REFRESHING CURRY IS A VIBRANT MIX OF FRESH INGREDIENTS — PINEAPPLE, TOMATOES, CUCUMBER AND CORIANDER (CILANTRO) — AND SWEET–SOUR SEASONINGS SUCH AS VINEGAR AND PALM SUGAR. THIS COMBINATION MAKES IT A GREAT SUMMER DISH: IT HAS A REFRESHING, SLIGHTLY SPICY AND SWEET FLAVOUR.

boneless pork leg	500 g (1 lb 2 oz), trimmed of excess fat
oil	1 tablespoon
garlic	3 cloves, crushed
brown malt vinegar	125 ml (4 fl oz/1/2 cup)
palm sugar (jaggery)	45 g (11/2 oz/1/4 cup) shaved
tomato paste (concentrated purée)	3 tablespoons
tomato	1, cut into wedges
onion	1, cut into thin wedges
pineapple	90 g (31/4 oz/1/2 cup), cut into chunks
telegraph (long) cucumber	1/2, halved lengthways, seeded, sliced
red capsicum (pepper)	1/2, cut into strips
jalapeño chillies (in brine)	21/2 tablespoons, chopped
spring onions (scallions)	2, cut into 5 cm (2 in) pieces
coriander (cilantro)	1 small handful leaves

Cut the pork into 3 cm (11/4 in) cubes. Heat the oil in a large saucepan over medium heat. Add the pork and garlic and cook for 4–5 minutes, or until pork is lightly browned.

In another saucepan, stir the vinegar, palm sugar, 1/2 teaspoon salt and the tomato paste over medium heat for 3 minutes, or until the palm sugar is dissolved.

Add the vinegar mixture to the pork along with the tomato, onion, pineapple, cucumber, capsicum, and jalapeños. Bring to the boil then reduce to a simmer and cook for 8–10 minutes, or until the pork is tender. Stir in the spring onions and coriander and serve.

Trim the pork fillet of excess fat and cut into neat cubes.

Add the cucumber and capsicum to the saucepan.

the perfect spice blend

A spice blend is a wonderful synergy of complementary spices. Whole spices — being the dried seeds, stems, bark or roots of particular plants — are dry-fried or roasted then finely ground to a powder to release their natural, aromatic oils. The most commonly known of these spice blends is curry powder. This mixture comes in several guises, forming the flavour structure for many curries, particularly Indian and Sri Lankan varieties. Although mainly used as the base flavour for cooked dishes, some spice blends, such as garam masala or five-spice, are often utilized at the end of the cooking process as a final aromatic addition to a dish.

For convenience, you will find most well-known spice blends in supermarkets and Asian food stores but, as with curry pastes, fresh is undoubtedly best. Fresh, whole spices retain many of the natural oils which carry flavour and aroma. If the spices are old or have been pre-ground for some time, they may have lost flavour due to age and exposure to air. So it is best to buy small amounts of whole spices and replace them as required.

To make your own spice blend, first dry-fry spices in a frying pan over medium–high heat for 2–3 minutes, or until fragrant. Ideally, dry-fry each spice separately to obtain optimum flavour as certain spices, depending on size and moisture content, will take longer than others to become fragrant. This process mellows the flavour of the spices, making for a well-rounded final result in your cooking. Allow the spices to cool then put them in a mortar and pound with a pestle until finely ground. You can also use a coffee or spice grinder. Store ground spices in a clean, well-sealed glass jar for up to 3 weeks, at which time the flavour will diminish rapidly.

lamb rizala .... serves 6

THIS RECIPE IS A STUDY IN HOW TO PRODUCE MELT-IN-THE-MOUTH TENDER, FLAVOURSOME MEAT. TRADITIONALLY, RIZALA FEATURED MUTTON, SO SLOW, GENTLE COOKING WAS THE IDEAL METHOD, BUT THIS APPLIES EQUALLY TO LAMB SHOULDER. THE YOGHURT FURTHER TENDERIZES THE MEAT, HELPING IT ABSORB THE AROMATICS.

onions	2, chopped
ginger	1 tablespoon grated
garlic	4 cloves, crushed
ground cinnamon	1 teaspoon
ghee or oil	3 tablespoons
lamb shoulder	1 kg (2 lb 4 oz), diced
plain yoghurt	125 g (4½ oz/½ cup)
chicken stock	250 ml (9 fl oz/1 cup)
crisp fried onion	40 g (1½ oz/½ cup)
red chillies	3, seeded, finely sliced
sugar	1 tablespoon
lime juice	3 tablespoons

Put the onions, ginger, garlic, cinnamon and 3 tablespoons of water in a food processor, or in a mortar with a pestle, and process or pound to a smooth paste.

Heat the ghee or oil in a heavy-based saucepan over high heat. Brown the lamb in batches and set aside.

Reduce the heat to low, add the onion paste and cook for 5 minutes, stirring constantly. Put the lamb back into the pan, and stir to combine, add the yoghurt a spoon at a time, stirring well to incorporate. Add the chicken stock, and crisp fried onion. Bring to a simmer, cover and cook over low heat for 2 hours. While cooking, skim any oil that comes to the surface and discard.

When the lamb is tender, add the chillies, sugar and lime juice, and cook for 5 minutes more before serving.

Garlic is a bedrock of most cuisines, and it is no different for the cuisines of India and Southeast Asia. In these regions, it is used in relishes and chutneys, vegetable dishes, stir-fries, roasted meats, breads, pickles and, of course, curries. Unmistakably pungent, its taste can vary from biting to mellow, depending on how it is prepared. There are many varieties of this hardy, bulbous herb, each differing in size, pungency and colour — Asian garlic is generally much smaller than Western varieties. Garlic is freshest in the summer when the bulbs are firm. Choose fresh, plump-looking bulbs with a white skin and store in a cool, open place.

chicken curry with apricots . . . . serves 6–8

THIS DISH IS A LOVELY BLEND OF SWEET, RICH APRICOTS AND MELLOW, ROUND SPICES SUCH AS CUMIN, TURMERIC AND CARDAMOM. WITH FRESH GINGER AND GREEN CHILLIES PROVIDING A BIT OF BITE, THE CHICKEN ITSELF SEEMS LIKE AN ALMOST INCIDENTAL INGREDIENT!

dried apricots	18
ghee or oil	1 tablespoon
chickens	2 x 1.5 kg (3 lb 5 oz), jointed
onions	3, finely sliced
ginger	1 teaspoon grated
garlic	3 cloves, crushed
long green chillies	3, seeded, finely chopped
cumin seeds	1 teaspoon
chilli powder	1 teaspoon
ground turmeric	1/2 teaspoon
cardamom pods	4, bruised
tomatoes	4 large, peeled, cut into eight pieces

Soak the dried apricots in 250 ml (9 fl oz/1 cup) hot water for 1 hour.

Melt the ghee or add the oil to a large saucepan, add the chicken in batches and cook over high heat for 5–6 minutes, or until browned. Remove from the pan. Add the onion and cook, stirring often, for 10 minutes, or until the onion has softened and turned golden brown.

Add the ginger, garlic and chopped green chilli, and cook, stirring, for 2 minutes. Stir in the cumin seeds, chilli powder and ground turmeric, and cook for a further 1 minute.

Return the chicken to the pan, add the cardamom, tomato and apricots, with any remaining liquid, and mix well. Simmer, covered, for 35 minutes, or until the chicken is tender.

Remove the chicken, cover and keep warm. Bring the liquid to the boil and boil rapidly, uncovered, for 5 minutes, or until it has thickened slightly. To serve, spoon the liquid over the chicken.

Sauté the chicken pieces in batches until browned.

Stir the spices into the onion mixture and cook until fragrant.

Add the chicken, cardamom, tomato and apricots to the pan.

thai beef and pumpkin curry . . . . serves 6

CURRIES ARE AS MUCH ABOUT AROMA AS THEY ARE ABOUT TASTE, BUT THIS CURRY ALSO CONTRIBUTES A WONDERFUL TENDER TEXTURE TO THE MIX. SOFT, SWEET PUMPKIN (WINTER SQUASH), MOIST, RICH BEEF AND CRUNCHY PEANUTS COME TOGETHER IN A SAUCE THAT IS HOT, RICH AND SWEET.

oil	2 tablespoons
blade steak	750 g (1 lb 10 oz), thinly sliced
musaman curry paste	4 tablespoons, ready-made or see recipe on page 17
garlic	2 cloves, crushed
onion	1, sliced
curry leaves	6, torn
coconut milk	750 ml (26 fl oz/3 cups)
butternut pumpkin (squash)	450 g (1 lb/3 cups), roughly diced
raw peanuts	2 tablespoons, chopped
palm sugar (jaggery)	1 tablespoon shaved
tamarind purée	2 tablespoons
fish sauce	2 tablespoons
curry leaves	to serve

Heat a wok or frying pan over high heat. Add the oil and swirl to coat the sides. Add the meat in batches and cook for 5 minutes, or until browned. Remove the meat from the wok.

Add the curry paste, garlic, onion and curry leaves to the wok, and stir to coat. Return the meat to the wok and cook, stirring, over medium heat for 2 minutes.

Add the coconut milk to the wok, then reduce the heat and simmer for 45 minutes. Add the diced pumpkin and simmer for 25–30 minutes, or until the meat and the pumpkin are tender and the sauce has thickened.

Stir in the peanuts, palm sugar, tamarind purée and fish sauce, and simmer for 1 minute. Garnish with curry leaves and serve.

Pour the coconut milk into the curry mixture and simmer.

Add the pumpkin and simmer until tender and sauce thickens.

chiang mai pork curry . . . . serves 6

THIS BURMESE-STYLE CURRY IS TYPICAL OF THE CHIANG MAI AREA IN THAILAND'S NORTH. IT IS UNLIKE THE MAJORITY OF FRAGRANT THAI CURRIES, IN THAT IT HAS A SPICIER, ALMOST INDIAN FLAVOUR. GENERALLY MADE WITH PORK, YOU WILL OCCASIONALLY FIND IT MADE WITH CHICKEN. THIS CURRY IMPROVES IF MADE IN ADVANCE.

chiang mai curry paste

coriander seeds	1 tablespoon
cumin seeds	2 teaspoons
dried long red chillies	2
salt	1/2 teaspoon
galangal	5 cm (2 in) piece, grated
lemon grass	1 stem, white part only, finely chopped
red Asian shallots	2, chopped
garlic cloves	2, crushed
ground turmeric	1/4 teaspoon
shrimp paste	1 teaspoon
ground cinnamon	1/2 teaspoon
pork belly	500 g (1 lb 2 oz), cut into cubes
oil	2 tablespoons
garlic	2 cloves, crushed
red Asian shallots	4, crushed with the blade of a cleaver
ginger	3 teaspoons grated
unsalted roasted peanuts	4 tablespoons
tamarind purée	3 tablespoons
fish sauce	2 tablespoons
palm sugar (jaggery)	2 tablespoons shaved

Dry-fry the coriander and cumin seeds in a frying pan over medium–high heat for 2–3 minutes, or until fragrant. Allow to cool. Using a mortar with a pestle, or a spice grinder, crush or grind to a powder.

Soak the chillies in boiling water for 5 minutes, or until soft. Remove the stem and seeds, then chop. Put the chillies, the ground coriander and cumin seeds with the remaining curry paste ingredients in a food processor, or in a mortar with a pestle, and process or pound to a smooth paste. Add a little oil if it is too thick.

Blanch the pork cubes in boiling water for 1 minute, then drain well. Heat the oil in a wok or saucepan and fry the garlic for 1 minute. Add 2 tablespoons of the made curry paste and stir-fry until fragrant. Add the pork, shallots, ginger and peanuts and stir briefly. Add 500 ml (17 fl oz/2 cups) water and the tamarind purée and bring to the boil.

Add the fish sauce and sugar and simmer for 1 hour 15 minutes, or until the pork is very tender. Add more water as the pork cooks, if necessary.